UNLESS A GRAIN OF WHEAT FALLS

Unless a Grain of Wheat Falls:
a Dying Father,
a Changing Son,
a Lenten Journey

Copyright © 2019 by J. B. Hobbs.

Cover photo by Dominik Martin. Used with permission.

Unless a Grain
of Wheat
Falls

A Dying Father,
a Changing Son,
a Lenten Journey

J. B. Hobbs

Contents

Acknowledgments and Foreword

There are all sorts of aphorisms about "best-laid plans" and how intended destinations change. And although these writings were originally started as a devotional, they too changed along the way.

It is a winding path that we follow.

These pages contain my reflections from a journey of several years, years during which my father was dying. Following the Lenten path that many have walked, I chronicle a particular experience and relationship. As I wrote, I found that the journey was also a story about how our experience and relationship with God changes over time.

I began writing our story three years after the death of my father and at the beginning of the season in the Christian calendar called Lent. Lent is a forty-day period observed in many Christian congregations. Traditionally, Lent was a period of preparation for a person entering the Christian church. This period of preparation ends on Easter Sunday with a rite of initiation known as baptism. It was in this way that the initiates journeyed through their own wilderness, a passage through a type of death into a new life.

These forty days remember, and in a way participate in the forty days of Jesus in the wilderness, the forty days and nights with Noah, his family, and the animals in the ark, and the forty years of wilderness wandering of the newly-freed Israelites as they journeyed from slavery toward the promised land. Forty is a number of completion, that a time is finished.

I began writing on Ash Wednesday. Using the Lenten Sourcebook as my guide, I wrote my way through Lent, through this time of emptying, preparation, and (hopefully) resurrection.

But as I wrote, my words became a meditation on my own images of God, on our journeys as individuals and as collected communities of faith, specifically through the lens of my own father's illness and death. My thoughts walked down the dirt road that led to the pig farm on which I was raised, over to the brick steps of the rural church in which my faith was formed, and eventually down a rough, paved gravel road to college and graduate school. My own particular journey has led me to writing, to working with people who are homeless, to the pastorate, to psychotherapy, and back to writing.

In my own experience as a son who has lost a father, and in my work as a counselor with many sons who have lost fathers, the death of the father for a son is an event that brings a time of questioning, of reconsideration, of being overwhelmed with what you "should" be as a man. No matter what kind of father is now gone, we feel a space where they lived in us. This loss is one that we feel emotionally, theologically, and psychologically.

Sigmund Freud, the father of modern psychology and himself an atheist, theorized in The Future of an Illusion (1928) that we project our idealized father outside of us, that we manufacture a deity based on this projection. Therefore this "Father God" to whom many pray is who we wish our own fathers to be, a fantasized form, made ideal in the image of God. And perhaps there is some truth there; I have met many men and women for whom their relationship with their father has clearly affected how they view God and their faith, especially in an environment dominated by an Evangelical branch of Christianity that prizes the image of God as father.

But perhaps this God as projected father was not the end for Freud either.

Mark Edmundson posits that at the end of Freud's life, in Freud's last published work Moses and Monotheism (1939), the psychoanalyst began to see the value in his own Jewish heritage, a heritage that included the revolutionary insight was denying the idol (or idols). In Judaism, there was to be no "graven image" of God. It is in this way, by denying any physical representation of God, that God moved inside of us. Instead of trying to encounter a being outside, we would plumb the depths of ourselves, allowing a non-represented, non-imaged God to be open and elusive. God was not out there; God was in us.

Perhaps this too is the way that our fathers are at first outside of us, instructing us, telling us the difference between a flathead and a Phillips-head screwdriver. The father is "larger than life" but slowly shrinks as we grow. And then one day, eventually, they leave us. And that leaving is initially felt like a loss, an absence. But then we hear their voice in our voice, sometimes saying the same sort of phrases that we heard our own father's say. We notice ourselves looking like them, acting as they did, even thinking thoughts that you are sure they thought too.

The leaving is not an absence in the end, but a transformation.

As for those who have walked along with me, I must first acknowledge my helpmate in writing and in life, my dear wife Dena. She endures my winding sentences and conversations and assists me in making a more concise sense of it all. We are both fortunate to be working with our agent Diana Flegel of Hartline in addition to the many other folks supporting us and our writing in our various communities of faith and life, including Dave Jones who assisted me in formatting this text so that it could be printed, and a wonderful community of writers at Medium. com. While these are more recent encouragers, my English professor and mentor Dr. Harry M. Bayne has been a voice of support from my early college days until now. And although there was much help with reading and revising along the way, the final text, including any errors, are mine alone.

In addition to those supporting my writing, I remain grateful for the clergy, fellow clinicians, and spiritual directors who have guided me along the way, especially the last two years of moving through the Spiritual Guidance Training Program through Shalem Institute.

My most cherished teachers, however, have been those who have invited me, as a clinician, to be a part of *their* journey through life and grief; it is an honor to sit with them in their vulnerability, as we try to move together toward transformation.

It is my hope, that in these writings there is some transformation here for you as well. Through these years of having a Lenten discipline of writing, I have tried to put some thoughts to paper each day; but as you may notice, there are days where there is nothing. At times I have struggled to fill in the gaps, but as much as some of us feel as if God can at times be hidden or absent, so have these days been empty.

I pray that as you read through these forty days, through this season of Lent (if that is how you use this text), that you allow yourself to journey through a period of preparation, then absence, and finally transformation.

For at the end of Lent is death.

But after that death, is a resurrection and new life.

"We come from a dark abyss, we end in a dark abyss, and we call the luminous interval life. As soon as we are born the return begins, at once the setting forth and the coming back; we die in every moment. Because of this many have cried out: The goal of life is death! But as soon as we are born we begin the struggle to create, to compose, to turn matter into life; we are born in every moment."

from *The Saviors of God* by Nikos Kazantzakis

"Spirit of my silence I can hear you
But I'm afraid to be near you
And I don't know where to begin
And I don't know where to begin"

from "Death with Dignity" by Sufjan Stevens

"We make the path by walking."

from Iron John by Robert Bly (but not original to him)

Carnival

The nearness of death tightens our hold on life. We squeeze it, grasping and gasping toward breath, toward movement, for loud noises instead of silence. We know silence will come. But for today, we make merry. We wear gaudy masks! We make noise because we can! This is life! Mardi Gras! Fat Tuesday!

The day before Lent begins, we celebrate. We move from a reminder of the gusto of life to a reminder of our shared mortality in the ashes, to the way in which none of us is permanent in this world. The exaggerated masks of the night before are removed. And with that removal, we relinquish the way that the mask may have obscured our viewing of the world, through small eye-holes versus a fuller, stranger vision.

Carnival is a moment of pause, taking careful note of the pleasure of a meal, of a drink, of touch, of the comfort of a bed. And then we are reminded of death, inevitable death. From dust we came, to dust we shall return.

But for today, "we will wear the mask."

I am reminded of the poem "We Wear the Mask" by Paul Laurence Dunbar. It describes the African-American experience of "wearing a mask" at times with the white folks in power when the slaves could not show their anger, their frustration. I know that with the privilege of my white skin, I did not grow up under that sort of oppression. Yet I do believe that many of us know the experience of wearing the mask. We know what it is like to be angry and hurt but to smile and defer nonetheless, to hide what we feel.

One of the symbols of Carnival is the mask. These masks are colorful and bright, covering the face. These masks are festive in spirit . . . at least on the outside. And along with the masks, we celebrate with our bodies, with these bright, plastic smiles, covering the hurt that exists inside. The gaudy purples and pinks, orange and yellow cover the grey underneath.

For the last few years, for me, this time of year has been like traveling through a strange land, wearing a mask as I go. Even though this is the time of Mardi Gras and Carnival, it was at the start of this season, several years ago, that my father was dying. The day before I checked him into hospice, just two weeks before Ash Wednesday, I took him to church one last time, to the white clapboard (now clean, vinyl siding) Southern Baptist church he had attended all his life. It was one last visit to that place, where the faithful gathered for worship. That church sits near one end of the road. If you travel just a couple of miles down that road, you will pass the home where my father was raised, then the home that he built, and the fields that he tended. At the other end of that road is an inpatient hospice facility.

The day after my father attended church one last time, we checked into that room in the hospice at the other end of the road. A few days later we gathered around a table in the common room and celebrated his birthday. With friends and family, we helped him blow out candles that would barely tremble under his now feeble breath. There were ice cream and cake. He ate a small amount, then returned to the hospital bed in his room. He would be the first of his siblings to die, although he was the next to the youngest one of them, even at 85.

And there were balloons. There was cake. There were M&Ms, an entire pack that was the color blue for his blue eyes. M&Ms had become his most recent favorite sweet snack.

And there were masks.

Our masks were our smiles, our singing of "Happy birthday to you." We smiled and sang, dancing the dance of celebration.

My father's mask was a swollen face, changed by the tumor that started near the back of his jaw, expanding and distorting his face as if he had been in a horrendous fight. Radiation has shrunk the tumor for a while, but the mass was returning.

The other tumor in his eyelid seemed to be returning as well. His eye that had been a clear and shining blue was now milky, shaded. Perhaps my father felt like he was looking through a mask too, just as we all were.

"Happy birthday to you; happy birthday to you," we sang. He played his part too, trying to blow out the candles, managing a bite of ice cream and cake, then returning to his room.

Celebration, then ashes.

Ash Wednesday

"What we call the beginning is often the end,
And to make an end is to make a beginning.
The end is where we start from."
                    —from The Little Gidding by T.S. Elliott

On March 11, 2011, my father died. It was a Friday, not a Wednesday. He would be buried on Sunday. Thomas Merton, a Trappist monk, wrote that the ashes of Ash Wednesday are properly thought of as Christ's victory over death. Ashes as victory. My father's death did not feel like a victory, but a prolonged sigh of defeat.

And that is what I remember most: that last long sigh.

I awoke that morning, around six o'clock, not sure why I had awakened. My mother was asleep in the chair next to his hospital bed there in the corner room of the inpatient hospice unit. I was beside the wall, a little further off, on a fold-away cot. There are probably 15 hospital beds there in that building, in separate rooms just like ours. There were nurses and staff and a common area in the middle of the building. There were flowers in the commons and a large, quietly-playing television, where a few people were taking breaks from sitting with a loved one who is struggling to breathe, struggling to live.

The room where we had slept was quiet. There was darkness, but the darkness was not complete. Unlike a hospital, hospice rooms are not filled with monitors and screens that light the room and the patient. It was a clinical room, easy to clean up and sanitize, with tiled floor, plastic molding around the floors, support rails in the bathroom, chairs, and nightstand on rollers so that you could move them quickly and easily. The room was clinical, but quiet and dim.

I suppose I awoke because my father's breathing had changed. His breath had been steady, although a bit shallow. It had not been a good night of sleep, with nurses coming in and out, although I am not sure why. I could tell he was close to death when we went through the motions of going to bed. He was barely responding to our words or touch. When his eyes were open, he did not seem to be looking at us any longer, just staring into the space in front of us, behind us, beside us. Perhaps it was the medications for pain and anxiety. From my own work in hospice, I know that some patients will look around, talking to deceased relatives, mumbling about a journey or having to pack to catch a train. The one who is dying sometimes communicates that they are leaving, but in ways that are true and not true at the same time.

But the truth was that my father was leaving.

One of the messages of Ash Wednesday is not a message of victory, but one where we hear, "Remember, you are going to die! Repent! The time is near!" Remember that you will leave this world!

On that Friday, at six in the morning, I awoke with just a hint of light in the room and the sounds of medical staff scurrying to complete the work of their shift. I woke up for that last moment, for my father's leaving.

As I stirred, I could tell that there was a change in him, a change in his breathing. I listened for a while, not knowing what the change meant, except that my father was pausing more between breaths. He would breathe in deeply. Pause. Then release a long, large exhale. Then pausing again. My mother was asleep in the chair beside him.

And then there was one last large exhale, a final emptying.

And I waited there, on that fold-up bed against the wall, just listening.

He was gone.

Friday after Ash Wednesday: Old Wood and Fences

There was a lot of old wood around the farm.

There was old wood that fixed fences. There was old wood that we used to make gates and chutes and ramps to guide the hogs from their pen up to the truck that would take them to market to be sold. We would hit them and holler at them from the dusty field near the pond around a maze of ramshackle wood to raise them five feet off of the ground into the back of a truck that would haul them to slaughter.

Having grown up during the Great Depression, my father learned that you used what materials you had. We even tried to reuse old rusty nails, if you could pull them out without bending the nail too much, you could use it again. On the farm, you did not buy anything new unless you absolutely had to.

So the fencing that held the pigs was often broken and repaired, over and over again. Barns were patched and re-patched. Machinery was broken and repaired. Gates that led in and out of different pens were often wired together to fix a broken hinge. The gates never did close the same way again.

As we move through those early stories contained in Genesis, we see a world beginning in goodness becoming broken and in need of repair. This breaking always seems to be our doing, because of our pride, somehow our fault. And in a stunning admission, God even goes so far as to say that God regretted ever making humans in the first place. It is as if

God had made some decision, saw how the decision played out, then wanted to rewind, to restart, and to perhaps create again. "I can do this better next time," God might say.

And despite saying out loud that God wanted to start again from the beginning, a clean slate, this God says, in the present here and now, that we will try again. In spite of our regrets and our sorrow at what creation had become, we try again, not from the beginning, but from where we are.

God starts again with one human, Noah, his family, the animals, and a large boat made of wood.

Having worked with the wood that was around me as I grew up, I have to assume that the wood that Noah used was stronger than what we had around the farm. Much of our boards were rotting and breaking, held up by rusty, slightly-bent nails.

The story of Noah during this season of Lent is about sin and redemption. It is about God's provision for us, that even when everything seems lost, we try again. That ark made of wood provides the way through, much as a cross made of wood is the image of Christian salvation. And even as Noah's ark traveled through the waters of the flood to reach salvation, the waters of baptism usher the new Christian into a new world, a new reality.

And in the ark, they were all together, all of creation, humans and all animals, packed in one boat. It is an intimate sort of journey, lion and lamb journeying together to their new life.

I admit I was never sure what my father and I were journeying toward. We did not talk much as we ambled around the farm, as we traveled in his pickup truck to the feed store to buy more "supplement" for the hogs, to buy large bags of seed to plant, to buy fertilizer. He wanted me with him, but he did not talk to me. He did not tell me his stories, although I suspected that the stories were there.

Strangely enough, he told my friend one of these stories as my friend was leaving for boot camp in the United States Army. I was not even present to hear it. My friend told me the story later. My father told my friend about how he came quite close to deploying to Normandy during World War II. This was a treacherous time and would have been a difficult passage. He did not say why, but instead, my father wandered around New York, caught pneumonia, and missed the journey. My father's story of World War II was not a story about a battle, but about wandering.

There are other stories that he never told me directly, tales of his alcoholic father, about him coming home from the Army to be with his father as his father died in the house next to the one in which I grew up. He never told me directly about how he administered the morphine to his father as he lay dying.

These are all stories that I did not hear; I would hear them later, through others.

It did not feel like I had a relationship with my father; it felt more like a journey that we were both on, packed in the same boat, perhaps eyeing each other cautiously, knowing that we were going somewhere, but not sure if it was going to be 40 days or 40 years.

And we were busy fixing broken fence along the way.

Saturday after Ash Wednesday: Wandering

The beginning of the Judeo-Christian story starts with a story of wandering, the story of Abraham.

Abram, as Abraham was previously known, was called by God to be the forbearer of God's people. But the story is never as easy as that. The journey is not a straight line. Despite God stating that he would be the father of multitudes, Abraham had not a single child to even begin to carry this promise forward. And so Abram traveled, moving from this place to that, wandering.

What can seem strange to us now is how Abraham's call is in a sense a call to wander, a call to travel away from your home. Scholars write that much of the Hebrew Scriptures were written after the time of the Babylonian exile, as a way of making meaning out of that time of exile. For the children of Israel, that time of exile in Babylon was a devastating loss. People were forced from their homes, marched to a much different place, enslaved among strangers, apart from what felt familiar and safe. They were a promised people that had made it to a promised land. But now there was this exile and desolation.

So then the wandering that had caused so much pain, so much dislocation of place and spirit, the wandering becomes a call in itself. The wandering is the calling.

Psalm 119 reads, "I am a sojourner on the earth, hide not your commandments from me." As Martin Buber writes about this psalm, he cites Rabbi Barukh in that there is some sense that God is like a second stranger with us, that this God is a stranger too, in a strange land. This strange God becomes our co-traveler.

At my office, in my work as a therapist, there is a children's book that I sometimes read to children who themselves feel like strangers, *A Color of His Own* by Leo Leoni. Leoni writes about a chameleon who also feels lost because his color does not stay the same. For other animals, there is a consistent color/home.

"Elephants are gray. Pigs are pink. All animals have a color of their own— except for chameleons."

So it was not to be for the chameleon. He tries and tries to fit here and there, thinking that if he stays in one place that his color will be consistent, that he will belong there. But he never finds his place, until he finds another chameleon. And instead of longing over and over to find a consistent color, these two decide to stay together and change together. And even though they do not have a "color of their own," they are together.

My own journey of faith has been one of a lot of wandering, sometimes away from God and sometimes drawing close. At times I can look back and see what from the advantage of hindsight appears to be a pattern. Yet, I am hesitant to call it a plan.

I grew up on one piece of land for my entire youth, but even then, I felt out of place. My parents were much older than the parents of my peers. I found myself reading books and listening to music that most of my classmates thought were strange. I did not necessarily feel at home, even though that land had been in our family for generations. It was home. That land is home. I know the language and the people and places. But there remained a discontentedness; there was something else.

So I wandered away from the land, not with a covenant, but because wandering is what felt like the right thing to do. And maybe there is a promise there somewhere in the wandering.

Maybe some of us are called to wander.

First Sunday of Lent: Wilderness

On this first Sunday where we officially enter the wilderness.

While Ash Wednesday is commonly seen as the beginning of Lent, that day is not the beginning. Ash Wednesday is the beginning of the Lenten fast, but the season of Lent officially begins on this first Sunday with a reading about Jesus entering the wilderness.

The wilderness is a place of wildness, a boundary place, a place of danger, a "thin place" where it seems that the heaven and earth meet, touch, and share the same space. What is usually so far apart, separate, is now close.

Although to call the wilderness a "thin place" may be too tame. For it is possible that something will grab you there, will reach right through that wall that separates the possible from the impossible. There is a ragged tear in the separation between order and chaos in the wilderness. And if we are truly in the wilderness, there is fear that you may not return.

Most of us do not have the experience of wilderness in our present reality. Most do not travel somewhere where we are unsure we will return. Yet, there are places in our minds and lives that feel like the wilderness. When we go to that place, *through* that place, we are changed. We do not come back the same if we come back at all.

For me, the landscape of grief has been a wilderness that I have traveled through, from which I have not emerged the same. I am changed. The death of a father is an event that changes you.

After my father's death, I remember walking down to the farm with my own children, who at the time of this memory were nine and ten years old. We were ostensibly walking my mother's dog, but the walk took us down to what was left of the farm and around the pond that sits there. When I was growing up there was some order to the place, structures that were present, barns, tall metal grain bins that held corn and wheat. There were long fences that held maturing hogs. There were faring houses that held sows and piglets.

Those structures were now gone, torn down. There is little there anymore. And the weeds are wild and have overgrown the walking paths. The land has changed in scale for me too. A collection of trees that was once a forest to me now seems like merely a patch of woods.

As my children and I were wandering around the edge of the pond behind what was left of a rickety shelter, they made the connection that this piece of land would one day be theirs. My son sees this as a wonderful prospect, so much to explore. He has the eyes of a young boy, looking for adventure out in the wild. My daughter is watching out for snakes.

And as for me, I see through the lens of my memory, the way that there is a wildness that has retaken possession of what was once tamed.

Monday of the First Week of Lent: Sad

My daughter asked me if I was sad. She knows that I am going to see my mother tomorrow, to have dinner with her after my day of work, driving 50 minutes to Dublin, to eat at Huddle House. Tomorrow is the third anniversary of my father's death.

I answered, "yes, some." She is a perceptive child. She watches. She feels what is happening around her. She knows that my mother will be upset and that this is the primary reason for the journey. I may or may not visit my father's grave. We made that visit just under two weeks ago on my father's birthday, leaving flowers there at the grave, flowers picked from our backyard at home. My mother had already been and placed three roses there, one for each year she had lived without him.

For me, the anticipation of his birthday and this time of year is worse than the event itself. It was the same with his death.

My father had first been diagnosed with a terminal illness seven years before he died. At that time, my wife and I were both pastoring churches in Effingham County, the next county over from Savannah-Chatham in Georgia. In addition to my work in a small, rural church, I had opened a private practice and was working part-time for a local hospice. My wife's church was larger, full-time, with many programs and responsibilities for her. In the same year of my father's diagnosis, we added two children to our family. Even though we were told that my father's prognosis would be one to two years, it took us about a year to effect a move closer to him and to my wife's family as well.

"One to two years," the pulmonologist had said. She diagnosed him with idiopathic pulmonary fibrosis. From my work in hospice, I knew that this would be a long, difficult journey. But the pulmonologist along with the rest of us may have underestimated just how sturdy my father was. He would not die from IPF. His death would be a full seven years later.

It was a strange irony that during my youth, my father often made a statement: "Well, your old man might not be around much longer." He had been worrying about and predicting his impending death for years. I remember wondering whether he would be alive when I finished high school. Then I was sure that he would not make it through my first two years of college. Then there was a transfer to another college, seminary, graduate school. And at each transition, the wondering was there. Would he still be around when . . .

But there he was . . . miserable, but there.

So even with the hard limit that comes with a "terminal diagnosis," my father's terminality was a question for me. After a period of decline, his lung capacity stabilized at around 65 percent. He would see the pulmonologist, who would test him. This 65 percent, give or take a bit, was an area that made him short of breath, but he did not decline further.

We seemed to have made an unspoken truce with death for now. No better. No worse. And I was not sad.

This truce came to an end when he was diagnosed with cancer. With this diagnosis, somehow I knew; I knew that he was truly dying. And this was when I felt sad.

My father was diagnosed with a rare type of cancer. My family was already scheduled to go away for several days to a cabin in North Georgia. His first surgery would be very soon, but we decided to go ahead with our trip. I bought some bourbon to sip around the campfire but instead drank too much that night. My children were too young to notice, but I spent what seemed like hours that night next to the toilet, vomiting, telling my wife that my father was going to die. I knew what was coming. It was the saddest I would be until his funeral.

The journey through all the treatment and eventually his death was worse than this life after. As a therapist, I know that there are many of us, especially in coping with long, drawn-out terminal illnesses, that grieve before the death. "Anticipatory grieving" we like to call it.

And this was the case with me. I feel that I shed many more tears before his decline and eventual death. The business of travel and treatment, of multiple surgeries, of chemotherapy and radiation, these were simply tasks to accomplish, steps to take. As the only child, it was my job (and with the gracious assistance of my wife) to go to appointments, to spend nights in hotels in Atlanta, to drive my parents this way and that, and to support my mother through these months.

And then one day, it was over.

Yet, the sadness is different on this side. Before my father's death, I went into a mode of doing, taking care of him and of my mother.

On the other side of all that busyness, there is a spaciousness to my grief; the emptiness gives you room to reflect, to consider.

"Am I sad today?" she asks me.

"Yes, some," I tell my daughter.

Tuesday of the
First Week of Lent: Ghosts

"Our Father, who art in heaven . . ."

That is hard for me to pray. Lately, it is hard for me to pray at all.

I find myself drawn to other ways of praying, praying without words, especially those prayers that allow me to eschew the image of a "heavenly father". One could hope that my image of father would be redeemed in some way by God as a father.

Yet the image of a father to me is one of someone who is distant, erratic, present, but then not reliable. It is an image of weakness, a strength of body (at least that seemed to be the case when I was young) that seemed capricious in its use. His body was used for hard work and occasionally showing such strength to a young son in order to be superior. My father would ask me to place my wrist in between his ring finger and middle finger. Myself as a young boy would comply. Then he would squeeze hard with his fingers against the bones in my wrist, causing my young body to writhe in pain, starting from my wrist and radiating out, helpless, unable to get free. "Your old daddy is strong, isn't he?!" I would slink away, not amused, not proud, clutching my wrist.

Then there were the times when he would ask me to make a phone call for him. In hindsight, I am not sure if this was anxiety about the call or a lack of confidence in knowing what to say. He asked me to call to make an appointment at the doctor's office. I was a young child; he was the adult. It was his appointment, not mine. He would tell me, "But you know how to talk to them; your old daddy doesn't." And although it was not hard for me to make the call, I would protest a bit, then end up doing what he had asked me to do. "Children, obey your parents," was what the Good Book said.

My father did not know how to talk to them.

I am not sure I know how to talk to God either, especially when my father is in the way.

I had dinner with my mother last night, at Huddle House in my hometown of Dublin. At some point, we talked about ghosts.

She went by the home where her mother had lived in the later part of my "Nannie's" life. My mother told me the story of how she drove by the old house, pulled into the yard to turn around, but also to get a better look. As she did, a woman must have been watching. This woman came out of the home toward my mother's car. The woman was African American. My mother remarked that this woman was picking up her dog, hurriedly, as if my mother, Caucasian, was going to try to take this stranger's dog from the yard. Race remains a sensitive issue in my hometown. This tension displays itself in gestures large and small, in the assumptions that those black and white make about the other.

My mother stopped and waved this woman over to her car. As the woman approached, my mother informed her that her mother had lived in the home. The woman then asked about my grandmother, telling her how she had seen a ghost from the window. The apparition was a woman taller than my mother and slender. The description in no way matched my short, stout, gray-headed grandmother, except for perhaps her piercing eyes. Nannie was always kind to me, but when I look at pictures of her, she never smiles.

The woman with the dog went on to talk about how she had heard footsteps moving from the kitchen to the den on a regular basis and a stray noise on the Venetian blinds. She said that her husband did not believe her at first, but then he heard it too. Now he too believes.

Ghosts.

I do not believe in ghosts.

Of course, I have heard stories of coincidences and eerie sounds and shapes. But, I do not believe. Maybe I spend too much time in other people's minds, knowing the tricks of perception that we unknowingly play on ourselves. We distort the world as it passes through our vision and our thinking. We see meaning in events where it does not exist.

But then there is the way that my father haunts who I am. I hear him in my voice at times, in the very words that I use, the thoughts that I think. I see him in my behavior, how like him I can be distant and irritable. For my own children's sake, I try to tell more stories about growing up, about my life, about what I have learned so far. I try to say more than he did, to give them more to hear than anxiety and worry and despair. I want them to hear more from me about hope and kindness and perseverance.

But then I am haunted by the words I do remember him saying.
"No one cares about me."
"If you are going to do something, do it right."
"Stop. Let me do that."

I do not believe in ghosts. I hear the stories, but I do not believe.
And I find it hard to pray.

Wednesday of the First Week of Lent: Grumbling

In my reading in scripture today, I encounter Jonah. You may remember Jonah as the story of the man who was swallowed by a whale. As a child, this was most of what I knew of the story.

Jonah's story is one of a calling by God to go preach to the people at Ninevah. He was to tell them to repent, to turn toward God, or be destroyed. Jonah did not want this particular job, so he did what many of us feel like doing when faced with a task we would rather not do: he took a boat sailing in the opposite direction.

But God will not leave him alone according to the story.

God sends waves and storms to the boat. The crew eventually realizes that Jonah is the reason for all their troubles, so they toss him overboard. And this is where the three days in the belly of the whale comes into the story. Despite Jonah's grumbling and reluctance, God saves him from drowning, preserves him.

There are times when I have felt reluctant to do some task that I knew had to be done. In my work, it is the difficult news of a diagnosis that must be delivered or entering into a discussion with an adolescent and their parents about the sexual abuse about which the parents have been unaware. There are times when I have been angry or scared, unsure of the outcome of a difficult conversation. Sometimes I do wish someone else would have these conversations, but here I am.

In this way, I have sympathy for Jonah. Part of me feels that Jonah's anger is justified. Can we not get angry when we are made to do something that we do not wish to do? Can we not say no to what we are asked to do?

Yet, I do feel more reluctance as of late, when after 40 years of life, my energy is not what it was. It is easy to commit to more than I can do, at work, at home, or at church.

The story of Jonah emerged in a conversation today with a patient. We talked about how Jonah was asked to share a gift, one that he was not comfortable or confident in sharing, but that is what he was called to do. And after such a display of reluctance, running the other way, traveling in the belly of the whale, when Jonah finally shared what God had asked him to share, that *gift was well-received*. This may have been the soft nudge that this person needed to be confident in their needed next step.

But I want there to still be some room for stubbornness, willfulness, wanting our own way and not what someone else (or God) would need from us. Maybe I spent too many years doing just that, being stubborn, trying hard to do what I needed or wanted to do, not what my father wanted or needed me to do.

My mother worked at J.C. Penney's department store as I was growing up. This meant a steady income and health insurance, two things that farming could not always guarantee. To be sure, when you sold a truck full of "number one" hogs, there was a nice paycheck. But then you might not deliver another load for a while. And a good bit of that money had to go back to the feed store, to diesel fuel, or to repair a combine. In many ways those who farm still feel quite dependent on what comes from the sky in terms of sun and rain, cold and drought.

Someone told me once that farmers are like gamblers, putting out their money, hoping to win this time.

So while my mother was at work, especially during the summers, I would often be with my father. I would fetch tools. I would hold baby piglets while my father took a razor blade and castrated them. I would spray pressurized water underneath the raised platforms where the sows and their new piglets were caged. The water washed away their offal, into a culvert and then out of the farrowing house. These were nasty jobs for the most part, not ones I wanted to do. But I did, with reluctance.

My reluctance was sometimes a verbal grumbling. Other times I simply doddled, took a long time, sprayed water in the same place for several minutes while my mind drifted. Or I did not do the job well enough. And my father would say his often repeated phrase, "If you are going to do something, do it right." And he would show me a pile of pig shit in the far corner that I had missed.

So I finished the job, spraying, watching it turn over, break apart, then spraying what was left down the culvert to the outdoors.

I did not feel better when the job was over. I did not exactly feel relief either. The job was simply done.

After preaching to the people of Ninevah, Jonah did not feel happy either. The people of that city turned toward God. God did not destroy them but instead had compassion. Yet, there was no pride in a job well done. Instead, Jonah was resentful. Jonah even says to God, "I knew this would happen! I knew you would be gracious and not destroy them!"

Then Jonah asks that he might die.

And God responds, "Is it right for you to be angry?"

I do not always care if it is right for me to be angry, but sometimes I am. Angry. Resentful. Critical. Frustrated. Why do I have to do this? Why can't someone else?

Jonah made himself a shelter. He made it, not God. But then God sent a plant to grow over the shelter and provide shade for Jonah. The story says that Jonah appreciated the coolness of the shade. Then God sent a worm to eat the plant. Next, God sent a "scorching east wind" toward Jonah, causing him great discomfort. With this wind and the hot sun overhead, Jonah felt as if he would faint. He again wanted to die.

God asks, "Is it right for you to be angry about the plant?"

Jonah responds, "It is. And I am so angry that I want to die."

We do not hear from Jonah again. God simply points out that Jonah did not raise this plant or destroy it. It was not Jonah's doing; this was God's doing. This is a radical dependence that most of us would rather not consider. We all want to govern our own outcomes, our own destiny.

Yet we do not control the rain or the sun. We do not make a plant grow or wither. And some of us get angry when someone else tells us what to do, even when they may be right.

Friday of the First Week of Lent: Individuation

I spent a lot of time being angry at my father.

From my own education, training, and experience, I know this is a common state for most adolescents. We figure out who we are in opposition to one of our parents, most commonly the same-sex parent. That parent is our model and foil. We see who we are by seeing how we are different from them. And often, pushing away from a parent, or the values of that parent, can feel angry, even violent.

It is a dreaded statement to hear during adolescence, "You are just like your father!"

The difficult part is seeing how much of that pushing back against my own father, how much of that effort was warranted. My anger was not about his overinvolvement in my life, as is often the case with the parents and adolescents with whom I work. My frustration with him was more about his absence, a lack of instruction or guidance. He wanted me there to work with him, but he never taught me the why or how of anything he did. He would ask for a Phillips-head screwdriver. I would get it for him. That was the extent of any conversation. And although he was known as an excellent mechanic with farm machinery, I could not tell you the first thing about what to grease and how often. I have no memory of him teaching me to drive a stick shift, yet I learned on an old hog-hauling truck.

So I ended up being angry at his absence, then giving up on his presence.

Yet, we are called to reconcile, to forgive. How does one forgive someone who is not there?

I remember my children's baptisms. The baptisms themselves were a bit of an event with my wife and I both serving nearby churches. Both congregations had been quite aware of our journey through adoption and then a difficult pregnancy. Our children arrived within a month of each other, although my daughter was a little over a year older than my son. Since my wife was an associate pastor, the baptisms would occur at her church, with her senior clergy performing the service.

I felt *off duty* that day, just a member of a congregation as opposed to leading it. I sat toward the front with my parents, holding my infant son, comforting him when he was getting fussy. I am not sure I would have wanted to be in that flowing christening gown either. My father was sitting beside me, seeming calm and settled in a way. He had never been to my wife's church, so typically he would have been a bit nervous, ready for this service to get started, to be over, and for him to be going home.

There was a pause as we waited, sitting toward the front of the church. My father in a deep blue suit, collared shirt, and tie. He sat with his hands propped on a cane that he sometimes used for walking. And in that space of that moment, he called to me as I held my son. I moved closer, and he leaned over to me and said, "You are a better father than I was."

I do not remember how I responded. I am not confident that I did respond, except perhaps with a half-smile.

On reflection, he seemed to be noticing and complimenting my attention to my son, perhaps wishing that he had done the same. In thinking about this moment now, there is a reconciliation of a sort, not direct, but clear. I remember being a bit lighter, easier after that morning.

We participated in the ancient ritual whereby my wife and I promised to share the faith with our children, that this water represented God's provision and acceptance of us, all of us, children and adults. That there is forgiveness for sin, for missteps, for mistakes, and that we are to offer this forgiveness to others, even those from whom we are separated by death.

And perhaps despite the history of anger and frustration, there is a way that I too have been able to forgive, to accept the father that I had, not a perfect one.

I have not been a perfect father either.

Second Sunday of Lent: Footsteps

Jesus said, "Whoever has seen me has seen the Father."

I am not my father. And I am not sure he wanted me to be. I remember walking in his footsteps though.

The soft grey dirt of the hog pen next to the pond was perfect for footprints. As we walked through that pen, hogs scattering, I would trudge behind him, watching where his worn, flat-bottomed workbooks would leave a perfect image in the soil. I would have to hop a bit to extend my legs to match his stride. But I would step/leap left-foot, step/leap right-foot, just behind him.

The old ones would say that you should not walk in someone's footprints because it will give them a headache. I am not sure what is meant by that. In our home, we had these books that were popular that contained folk remedies and sayings. For instance, do you have a headache? Take a hair from your head and place it under a rock. According to this book, that would relieve it.

I never quite believed in that. Now, my mother, she would say that she was "not superstitious, just cautious."

The walking in my father's footsteps was in part trying to match his stride. I would note the difference in the size of his feet and mine, the length of his stride and my efforts to match it. Another part of me knew what the old ones said, that this might give him a headache. I wonder if the boy in me, trying to grow, trying to match and exceed my father in some way wanted to give him a headache.

He would not be the first father to say that his son was causing him pain.

My father was not a teacher. Other than telling me the difference between a Phillips-head and flathead screwdriver, there was not much on the farm that he would explain. I wonder at times whether my father's lack of instruction about his work was so that I would *not* walk in those footsteps.

He worked hard. He would get up early, go down to the barn, coming back about the time I was heading to school. He would go to breakfast, taking care of some business in town, buying feed, diesel fuel, a part for a plow, then it was back to the pigs or the fields. He would come home, most of the time, for lunch. Then depending on the time of year, he may go back to the fields until it was dark.

This was a path that I am not sure he wanted me to follow. It was a path that I did not intend to follow.

But here I am in the present, overworking myself many days, starting early with a phone call, or a chart to finish or letter to write, seeing patients from morning until evening, taking phone calls in the middle of the night at times. And by the nature of my work, I cannot tell my children much about what I do. Even though my father and I work in very different ways, some patterns of walking continue.

So what did Jesus mean when he said these words?

"When you have seen me you have seen the father."

We see the face of God in many ways. There is the face that Jacob sees in Genesis when he wrestles with God, then later sees this same face in the forgiveness that comes from his brother Esau. Many saints will tell you that they have seen the face of Jesus in the poor that they serve.

My father is in me. And I am in my son too. From the time when he was an infant, people in the church that I served would jokingly say, "Well . . . you can't say he's not yours!" And there is most certainly a glint in his eye if he is trying to get away with something that he knows he should not do. Now, as he moves into adolescence, he challenges ideas, craves knowledge and understanding, and sometimes makes my head hurt.

I am not sure that I want my own son to walk the steps that I have walked, but there he is, challenging me at times, not trying to cause me pain, but seeing if he can match my steps . . . or go further.

Monday of the Second Week of Lent: Decay

There has been a conflict for me these last few years about the coming of spring. This time of year is also filled with reminders of decline and death. Yet, there are ways in which death and the emergence of new life are a part of each other. One needs the rich soil, the compost, the decaying of once-living material to become the place in which the new-living seeds can grow.

There was a poem that I encountered that seemed to speak to the conflict, "Spring" by Edna St. Vincent Millay. It reads:

> To what purpose, April, do you return again?
> Beauty is not enough.
> You can no longer quiet me with the redness
> Of little leaves opening stickily.
> I know what I know.
> The sun is hot on my neck as I observe
> The spikes of the crocus.
> The smell of the earth is good.
> It is apparent that there is no death.
> But what does that signify?
> Not only under ground are the brains of men
> Eaten by maggots.
> Life in itself
> Is nothing,

An empty cup, a flight of uncarpeted stairs.
It is not enough that yearly, down this hill,
April
Comes like an idiot, babbling and strewing flowers.

As I read this poem, the line about the brains of men being eaten by maggots, it hits me. My father lies underneath the ground, decaying.

As I write, I am inside this house, warm. And on this cold, wet morning, my father remains, as he has for three years now as of the day on which I write this, underneath the ground, in a vault, in a casket, decaying.

The place where he is buried is in the cemetery across the road from the church that he attended for his entire life. The church formerly housed a school, which is where my father and many others received their early education. The school eventually closed while the church continued.

The cemetery sits in a corner of our farmland with a chain-link fence surrounding it. These fields have at times grown wheat, corn, soybeans, and peanuts. Occasionally sunflowers would be planted in a few rows to attract dove in the fall for hunters.

Just a few years before my father died, he donated an additional acre to the church for the cemetery. As the church has grown, so had the need for a place to bury the dead.

My father is now one of those dead, having been buried in land that he would harrow, plow, and plant. But we do not bury our dead in such a way that they can grow again.

In Job (14:7–12), it is written that there is hope for a tree; it blooms again. The trees spring forth their "little leaves". In our front yard, miles from that field where my father is buried, this is the time of year when the daffodils peek out from the soil, grow to their full stature, then burst with bright, yellow blooms. These are bulbs that my daughter and I planted together, tended, eventually pulled apart and planted again.

From my other forays into the small scale of composting and vegetable gardening, I learned to work the soil, to turn the dark organic matter. That rich, dark, decayed matter became what nurtured our tomatoes and peppers, squash, and cucumbers. Decay leads to new growth.

But not so with my father. He is under the ground, in a vault, in a casket, just decaying.

At the time of this writing, it seems to be this way with my relationship with God. In Protestant circles, especially evangelical ones, we tend to talk about a "personal relationship" with God. It is as if you take a walk together, talking about your day, sharing that joke you heard at lunch. This language represents a relationship that is nurtured, that feels close. And while there were times in my youth where I felt a closeness, that relationship has shifted.

I tell myself I have a quieter, more staid faith. But at times I think that is just a mealy-mouthed way of saying that I just walk through my faith, as if by rote. I know it is a part of me, my heritage, my worldview. It just no longer feels alive.

And I wonder if my faith too is in the earth, in a vault, in a casket, decaying.

Or is it like the tree?

Tuesday of the Second Week of Lent: Straight Rows

"Look at that! Look at how straight those rows are," my father would tell me.

There is an African American spiritual that speaks to how faith and farming go together.

> When you plow don't lose your track.
> Can't plow straight and keep a-lookin' back.
> If you want to get to heaven, I'll tell you how,
> Keep your hand right on that plow.
> Keep on plowin' and don't you tire.
> Ev'ry row goes higher and higher.
> If that plow stayin' your hand,
> Heads you straight for the promised land.
> Keep your hand on that plow, hold on.
> Hold on, hold on.
> Keep your hand on that plow, hold on.

There is truth in this old hymn. My father could tell you that. You keep your hand on the plow. You hold on and on.

He was proud of how he held on . . . and he held on, to this life, for 85 years. He was also quite proud of the straightness of those rows that he would dig into the dirt with the plow.

"Look at that! Look at how straight those rows are," my father would tell me.

My memory has me sitting on the right side of his truck, a 1984 Ford, blue and white exterior, my father sitting on the left. We would drive around the fields at times, times when we were waiting for growth, for tiny soybean plants to pop out from the soil. Sitting. Waiting. More often than not my head was buried in a book. There was only so much staring at the lay of the land and the interior vinyl landscape of that old truck that a young boy could do.

"Son," he would say, urgently, as if something important was happening. I would peek out from behind the pages.

"Look at that! Look at how straight those rows are," he would tell me.

And I would take my gaze from the straight lines of words on a page, up the lines of the armrest of the door of the truck and out of the window, down acre after acre of field. From my perspective, you could look straight down the row of plowed and planted dirt. There were small but distinct lines leading away from where we were parked to the far side of the field. He was proud of the straightness of those rows and wanted me to see, almost as if he wanted me to tell him that he had done a good job.

It struck me as strange that a father to seek the approval of his son.

"Look at what your old daddy did!"

As I have grown older, having my own son now, there are accomplishments that I want to share with him. Perhaps I want him to be proud of me, to see what his "old man" can do. But I hope I do not need his approval. After all, the way to heaven is the "straight and narrow," right? Put your hand to the plow and don't look back.

I think that my father did a lot of looking back. He drove slowly because he had been in a terrible accident as a young man, hitchhiking back home from the Army. Having been raised with an alcoholic father had changed him, in ways that make you crooked, bent, difficult to straighten out again. He did not exactly have a father who noticed him, who would have told him "good job".

He was proud of those straight rows because he could see that it was done. There is something about doing a job and doing it right. If you do what you are supposed to, it does feel a bit like it is leading to heaven.

But don't look back; keep your hand on the plow.

40

Wednesday of the Second Week of Lent: Healing

Jesus asks, "Do you want to be healed?"

It is 38 days until Easter. There were 38 years that the man at the pool of Bethsaida had lain there, waiting to be healed, according to John 5:1–15. There were also 38 years between the year of my birth and the year of my father's death.

Living with my father was difficult in ways. He worked very hard, as a farmer. There were expectations that you would do the same. He was full of complaint and suffering, some of which was aches of the body, arthritis. But there were those times too where he would comment that no one knew how he suffered . . . or no one cared how he suffered. There were sufferings of mind and spirit as well.

And oh how he wanted to be healed!

I cannot speak about what happened prior to my birth. My father was 48 when I was born. As early as I can remember, there were frequent visits to this or that doctor. He was looking for some cure for what he always described as *pain*. He was "just an old farmer" though, so he would say he was "tremblin'" and "wringing wet with sweat." He would see general practitioners, internists, at one point thinking he was possibly diabetic. There were pain specialists and chiropractors. He was quite proud when he was sent to Augusta, Georgia, home of one of the best medical schools in our state. He would beam with pride when he would tell about how the doctor told him that he had the worst case of arthritis that the doctor had ever seen!

One of the stranger memories that I have is driving to Dothan, Alabama from our home. It was about 200 miles through small towns in both states arriving at a doctor's office in what seemed to be a partially renovated house. I must have been ten years old at the most.

The first room had a television with a videotape where the procedure was explained. Somehow what would happen next would "clean" my father's blood of the particles in it that were harming him. The procedure itself would take several hours and would have to be repeated many times. The room was dark and seemed poorly kept, but my father believed . . . or at least he was willing to try to believe if it made him feel better. I suppose if you are in enough pain, you will try nearly anything, even waiting to jump into a pool that is supposed to heal you.

If you ask me now, I would speculate that the procedure that my father had was chelation, a "cleansing" of the blood that has even been used on children with autism, although there is little evidence behind such claims. But logic does not stop you from trying to get in the pool when you have been waiting there for 38 years.

For this man who could not walk in the gospel of John, waiting at the pool at Bethesda, his complaint was that no one would help him. The story was that an angel would come to the pool, stir up the water, then the first one in the pool would be healed. The story sounds cruel in a way for those who need healing the most would be the least likely to get to the pool first. So this man waited by the pool and complained that no one would help him.

Jesus learned that this man had been wanting to be healed for 38 years. With little other background information, Jesus walks up to the man and asks, "Do you want to be healed?" While it may seem a silly question, there are often reasons to remain sick, known to the person who is ill or not. Sometimes imagining a life without illness, especially after so many years of structuring your life around an illness, just the thought of being "cured" is both wonderful and frightening. Our identities can become built around many aspects of who we are. Illness is surely one of these too.

But Jesus asks, "Do you want to be healed?" And it is a valid question for any of us when the possibility of change, of healing, is offered.

There are wounds in my life that I am not sure I would want to be taken away at this point. They have shaped me. I have seen goodness emerge from pain. But our wounds and our pain also have the ability to distort us, to cause us to turn inward, focusing only on the pain.

But Jesus asks, "Do you want to be healed?"

"Take up your mat and walk," Jesus told the man. And the man did.

Thursday of the Second Week of Lent: Homeless

I was in college when I spent my first night in a homeless shelter. It was not exactly by necessity.

I was working as a stringer for our student newspaper making $7 a story and wanted to be staff, which would mean I would make a whopping $14 per story. I wanted the "fluffy features" beat, which typically meant human interest stories around town and campus. My editor decided that the position would be mine if I would do a series on homelessness in Athens. The series included a night in a homeless shelter.

So my first night in a homeless shelter was not exactly a necessity; it was chosen. Of course, I did not tell my mother until after that night was over.

My hair was already a bit long and unkempt. In preparation, I did not shave for a few days. I had called ahead and met with the captain of the Salvation Army homeless shelter. That night, after I was checked in, the captain let the staff person know that I was there. My story was that I was a college student whose roommates had kicked him out of their apartment.

"You don't belong here," one man told me the next morning.

We were all packing our belongings as it was time to leave for the day. He gave me a sample-sized deodorant as he made his pronouncement. I am not sure what he thought about me at that moment, other than what he communicated with his gift. The assumption under his statement, "you don't belong here," is one that most of us have had in our minds, that there are those who deserve to be in the situation that they are in and there are those that do not. For some reason this man had me among those that did not; I wonder if he thought of himself as someone who deserved to be where he was.

As I had entered the shelter, I carried a few items in an old ALICE pack that I used for my school bag. So at varying points, I sat in a common room with an English anthology, reading part of Thoreau's Walden and the "quiet desperation" most people live their lives in. I ventured to the porch to smoke, which is where the real conversations would happen. One older man had been fixing a woman's porch that day and had fallen. He groaned and complained that he thought he had broken a rib or two, "but there's nothing to do about it."

That night, I put my shoes in my ALICE pack and slept as much as I could with the straps threaded through my arms, my head resting on the pack. Throughout the night, the man who had been injured that day would turn, groan "God damn it," and then return to sleep. In the morning, we would all wake up, wander into the bathroom, packing up what we needed for the day.

I know that I do not know what it is like to be homeless. Later that day, I would return to my apartment, shower, go to class. I did not belong there.

But it could have been me. It could have been any of us.

There are reminders through this season of Lent to give to those who are poor, to those who have less than we do. There are calls to fast, not for ourselves, but to give the money we would have spent on that meal to someone who does not have anything to eat.

When we have ease in our lives, benefits that were given to us, it is easy to fall into the thought that "I belong here" through some intrinsic quality or favor of God. But Jesus is continually chastising those who have more when they do not share with those who have less. He was criticized by the religious leaders for spending time with tax collectors, prostitutes, and sinners. These were people that were likely told that they deserved their place in life.

So we give to others to follow Jesus's example of service, of servant-hood. And as is a theme of Lent, we remember our own sinfulness, our own brokenness, because none of us "belong" any more than anyone else.

Friday of the Second Week of Lent: Talons

While the spiritual journey can conjure images of winding wooded paths or labyrinths, of churches and spaces where we felt at home with God, that is not always the path.

Many spiritual writers will refer to "dark nights of the soul," experiences in which God seems absent, hiding. Just as harrowing are those moments where God is present but perhaps we are not wanting to do what God has called us to do. This hearkens back to so many stories from scripture, from Jonah to Moses, to many of the prophets.

Yet, we do not usually think of Jesus in this way.

The few stories we have of Jesus as a young person are of a child who knows his purpose from early on, already conversing with the religious leaders in the temple as a boy. This is the Jesus who does not struggle, from birth through death, floating through all of this to resurrection and a triumphant return to heaven.

But there is another image that speaks to me.

Nikos Kazantzakis writes in his *The Last Temptation of Christ* of Jesus as a youth, feeling the call of God on his life. This call of God is represented as the talons of a mighty bird, flapping around the young Jesus, clawing at his skull, an image that is bloody, shocking. The clawing of God challenges us to think about Jesus's freedom as a human being, even as an adolescent, and whether he could choose or not choose God's calling. God's call is seen as violent, disturbing this boy who only had intentions of learning the trade of his father, learning to work with wood and nails. And yet, God comes, clawing at him, puncturing his scalp.

Thomas Merton writes in *Thoughts in Solitude* about approaching God in compunction and adoration. This word, *compunction*, has to do with feeling guilty about something we have done or maybe something we should do.

Now I spend a lot of time in my work in therapy helping people relieve themselves of feeling guilty over events that were in no way their responsibility. But there is something about the spiritual life that involves a sort of puncturing of our lives, of our selves, a piercing that does not allow us to have illusions before God. That puncturing is often not pleasant; it could feel like God has talons sinking into our scalp.

Fridays in Lent are not intended to be pleasant. Many will fast from meat (except for fish) on Fridays throughout the year, and there have been traditions of fasting more completely on Fridays during Lent. The call to abstain, to feel some sort of hunger or pain, is a call to feel as Jesus must have felt.

Jesus on the cross is not floating above the world; he is fully human in that moment. He felt pain. He bled. He died.

The call to follow Jesus is not a call to success and prosperity. It often involves pain and suffering. That is the path.

The call is to "take up your cross and follow me". That will also mean leaving aspects of our own pride and ego, of who we want others to think that we are, of who we feel we should be for others. Being open with God, knowing that there are grace and love there, means that we can be punctured, that our illusions will be torn.

This puncturing may also be our ideas about who God is. Because when God looks too much like us, when we find that we are comfortable with God because God only likes who we like and dislikes what we dislike, then when God does show up, we may find ourselves afraid and bleeding, feeling punctured by the talons of a mighty bird.

Saturday of the Second Week of Lent: Leaving

Sometimes we have to leave in order to make way for the return.

Martin Buber wrote: Once, on the eve of the Day of Atonement, Rabbi Zusya heard a cantor in the House of Prayer chanting the words: "And it is forgiven," in strange and beautiful tones. Then he called to God: "Lord of the world! Had Israel not sinned, how could such a song have been intoned before you?"

Sometimes we have to leave in order to make way for the return.

The last time that I felt like I truly left faith was when I was in seminary. You could certainly argue that seminary challenges your ideas about God, this text that we call scripture, about who Jesus is and was, but those ideas were more exciting than challenging. But it was the people of God, especially the leaders of faith, those are the ones that I find the most challenging.

So being in my late adolescence, my frustration was directed at my theology professor and at the seminary president. As I have gotten older, I can see how either one of them could be a "stand in" for my own father. I wanted their blessing; I wanted my own father's blessing.

This was also the first time that I saw a therapist, needing help to process my own anger, and how I was turning that inward. Those who work in clinical areas may have heard the old truism that anger turned inward leads to depression. There are times when we are angry and do not allow that anger to be expressed. Perhaps the object of our anger is absent. Maybe that object is quite good at deflecting or avoiding or leading you to question whether you should be angry at all. And so you question yourself.

Maybe it is your fault after all.

Maybe you should leave.

The prodigal son does leave, without much of a reason given. We tend to place a lot of blame on him for how he uses his share of his father's wealth in the city, that he squanders it on "wild living". This story is almost always seen as blaming of the son, that he left with every intention of spending all of that money. We feel a sort of smug judgment when this prodigal ends up broke and broken, eating with the pigs.

But I wonder.

Did he leave because of something else?

What are the myriad reasons that any of us leave? Sometimes we take our share with us, no intention of ever returning. To be sure, it is the height of adolescent hubris that we sometimes think that we do not need them.

"Give me what I deserve so I can finally be done with you!"

But in the parable of the prodigal son, the father waits for him. Henri Nouwen rightly tries to rename this story to emphasize "The Love of the Father" instead of "The Prodigal Son". Because the emphasis, and Jesus's point in telling the story, is on the father who waits at the end of the road, patiently, expectantly, with love.

Maybe this father knew that the son would eventually come to a place where he realized his need of family, of faith, of heritage. One wonders whether this father had been on a similar journey, of resistance and return, a sort of Heideggerian thesis and antithesis leading to a synthesis.

Maybe this father knew that one has to be patient with those who are angry with you, accepting that some of the anger is deserved, that some of the anger comes from the hurt of rejection.

For me, I left because I did not feel that there was a place for me. I felt outside and alone; I took my degree and left. I would never be Baptist again. And then I became United Methodist, but that father rejected me too. I was less angry when I left that time, but leaving was still the right thing to do.

And each time, the leaving did not only feel like leaving a particular flavor of Christianity in the United States. It felt like leaving God.

In reality, each exit was more like leaving an old idea of God, a conception that was now limiting or did not fit anymore. I took what I had received, what I felt like was rightly mine, and I left.

And is that sin?

And if the leaving is a sin, do we need such "sin" as this to provide the opportunity for forgiveness and reconciliation, not just with people, but with God?

"Had Israel not sinned, how could such a song have been intoned before you?"

Third Sunday of Lent: Leaving It Behind

"If you drink this water, you will thirst again," Jesus tells the Samaritan woman in John 4. It was the middle of the day when she had come to fill her water jar; it is assumed she was avoiding contact with others. No one goes alone, in the middle of the day, to get water from the well.

A scarcity of water is not a typical experience, not for any of us who have lived in a first-world country in the last fifty years. My father used to brag about how they had "running water" when he was a child. With a gleam in his eye, he would say, "I *ran* to the well to get it, filled up the bucket, and *ran* back!"

My own father knew what it was like to have a well. Even earlier in my family's history was a fellow named Milton S. Jones. Every year at our family reunion, I would be reminded that Milton S. Jones had the first artesian well in Laurens County. That did not impress me much at the time. Since then, I understand that this meant that one did not need the labor of pumping in order to draw the water up out of the ground. In addition, an artesian well provides water that is naturally filtered and pure for drinking. Both of these qualities meant an abundance of clean water, easy to retrieve.

There's no indication that the well from which this Samaritan woman drew water was in any way easy. As Jesus talks with her it becomes clear that there her life had been easy. He tells her that she has had five husbands and that the man with whom she is currently living is not her husband. To put this in the context of that time and place, these multiple husbands were less about her "sin" and more a sign that she had been thrown away, multiple times; her only way of supporting herself being to attach herself to another man that may misuse her.

This was a woman who had been belittled and demeaned, and Jesus was talking to her.

To have someone, anyone talk to her must have felt like water in a desert for this woman. It was life-giving for someone to see her, to acknowledge her, to know her deeply, and still talk with her. This is what Jesus does for her.

And he talks about water.

As my father and I would get ready during the summers to go down to the farm, it was not water that we would pack in a gallon-sized thermos. More often than not it was sweet tea with lemon. I am confident that I did not sweat as much as he did, as I did not work as hard as he did. But when we were out in a field, far from a water hose, that gallon thermos of sweet tea was water in a Georgia desert. It was enough to keep us going a little longer, my father usually plowing or planting, with me sitting in the truck with bags of seed, moving it occasionally to catch up with my father so that we could dump another bag of seed into the hoppers on the back of the planter. In the morning on the days we were planting, there was no way we would have left that thermos.

Maybe that is why the woman at the well's action stands out to me: after Jesus promises her living water, this water after which she will never thirst again, this one who had been so abused understands what Jesus is offering.

And even though she had come to the well to draw water, she leaves her water jar behind.

Tuesday of the Third Week of Lent: Sweet Stories

There is something in us that likes a story to have a sweet ending, even the most brutal, bloody stories. But that is not always the way.

One of the stories that arises during my own readings in Lent is the story of Samson. This is a story about which I can still conjure the images from the picture Bibles of my childhood: Strong Samson, defeating the enemies, tearing the lion apart with his bare hands. The images in that book for children are sanitized compared to what you find in the story.

Judges 14:14, "Out of the eater came something to eat. Out of the strong came something sweet."

This riddle is drawn from the part of the story where Samson goes to find a wife. He searches among a foreign people, the Philistines, with whom he was constantly battling. This nomadic people always seemed to be fighting others for their place in the land.

Samson finds a woman that he "is pleased with". On one of his trips to marry her, he is attacked by a lion. In the story, he rips the lion apart, "as he would have a young goat". Yes, this is not the later image of the gentle Jesus holding a tiny lamb. This is a bloody tearing of flesh, a brutal struggle for life.

Samson bests the lion, leaving the carcass torn in two. On a later trip, he passes by this same place only to find that bees have made a hive in the decaying flesh of the lion. There were honey and honeycomb. Samson reached in and tasted its sweetness.

"Out of the eater came something to eat; out of the strong came something sweet."

If you read the full story, you will find that Samson is boastful, telling a group of thirty of these Philistines that he will give them a new set of clothes if they can tell him the answer to his riddle within one week. They, in turn, pressure their fellow countrywoman, the woman that Samson has come to wed, to find the answer. She begs and cajoles until finally on the last day, Samson tells her the answer.

She tells her fellow countrymen, who then tell Samson the answer to his riddle. But instead of something "sweet" happening, Samson goes to a neighboring town, kills thirty men there, taking their clothing. He makes good on his promise to give these men a new set of clothes. He fulfills what he said he would do, although in a horrible and violent way.

I do not remember this part in the children's bible.

The story of our lives is not always the sort of story that you tell children, or at least the kinds of stories that we think we should tell children. There is also a way in which we prefer stories of faith that have a "sweet" ending, moving quickly past the struggle, ignoring some of the difficulty that lay in between the beginning of the story and the "sweet" ending.

This is one of our difficulties with this season of Lent. It is not as short as Advent with its story of the birth of a baby at the end of the labor. Lent is long and plodding. This season asks us to look at ourselves, at the pain (sin) in our own lives. This is pain that we have sometimes caused. It is also often the pain caused by others, intentionally or not. It is still pain. It is still sin. It still hurts.

And even though this season ends at Easter, at resurrection, we are asked to sit with this pain for a good, long while. We cannot ignore it or wish it away. Moving swiftly to resurrection, toward a "sweet" ending, runs the risk of ignoring bloody horrors in between. It is part of the journey of faith to be present with this suffering, with our own suffering and the suffering that we have caused.

Wednesday of the
Third Week of Lent:
After

Today, it has been four years since my father died, four years since I awoke to hear the change in his breathing at about six in the morning, four years since I heard my father's last breath.

Lying several feet from him on a fold-up cot, I simply listened as he left us and a sense of emptiness filled the room.

My mother was sleeping in the recliner next to his bed. I slowly got up, walked over to him and kissed him on the forehead. He was motionless. I told him goodbye and that I loved him. Then I gently woke my mother and told her that he was gone.

Today is a Wednesday, with dark mornings returning since the time change a few days prior. I am having difficulty getting up in the mornings, although I cannot distinguish how much is due to the time change or due to this anniversary. I have felt tight in my neck and back. I have noticed that I am vaguely distant from wherever I am. I don't think that anyone notices. I hope that no one notices.

I traveled to my home to have dinner with my mother. After I took her back to the home in which I was raised, I stopped by my father's grave, just one-half mile away. The cemetery sits catacorner to the church. My friend's father would joke that one day he was going to graduate from his Sunday School class to "that other class across the street" cocking his head toward the cemetery.

As it was a Wednesday evening, there were activities at the church earlier: prayer meeting, choir practice. Now, it is dark with cars and trucks leaving.

On Wednesday nights when I was a young boy, I would play with friends during choir practice, as we waited on our mothers. We would throw balls against the wall of the fellowship hall. We practiced lighting matches and throwing those. We shared the worst curse word that we had heard our father's throw out in front of us. One early evening while roaming the grounds, we found a decayed Easter egg from a year (or possibly two) before; this gave us a true understanding of what it meant for someone to say, "Last one is a rotten egg!" The smell was awful.

And sometimes, we would dare each other to go into the cemetery.

As a child, I could not have imagined going into that cemetery at night, alone. Even as a boy with the threat of losing face in front of my peers, I would not have gone. No one did. But tonight, on the anniversary of his death, I wanted to go by my father's grave.

I had imagined talking to him. Saying whatever you say at a grave. "I miss you. Mom misses you terribly. The kids are doing fine." I thought of talking to him as if he was there, but then we never had those conversations when he was alive. The words between us were always brief. As I got older and was driving, he would say, "Hold them in the road!" as I was leaving. I am not sure where that phrase emerged; I was not driving a pair of horses to market.

I drove my car alongside the chain link fence as my headlights reflected off of the polished marble. Yet as I parked, exited my car, entered the fence and walked to the graveside, I just felt blank. No words. No tears.

I squatted for a while on the coping around the gravesite, looking at the date on my father's stone, noticing the stone that we had already laid for my mother with her birthday but without a date of death. Just blank there too.

As I stood up again, I felt a long exhale emerge from me.

This is also a part of loss: the memory, the exhale, and the emptiness after.

Thursday of the Third Week of Lent: Body

I remember my father's body.

For the longest time he had the arms of a farmer, the sort of building up of the fiber of muscle from pushing and pulling, from striking with a hammer, from picking up bags of seed, from lifting the connection point of a plow to meet the tractor so that you could even begin your work. He was strong.

I remember his skin, the patches of darkness, the deep tan of his arms from sitting atop a tractor, in the sun, pulling the iron blades through the soil, upending weeds in between the growing soybean stalks. His arms, neck and face were dark, but when he peeled off the sweat-soaked t-shirt, his chest would be a pale white.

His hands were callused and hard. I do not remember holding that hand often as a child. More often I remember seeing it bloodied, hit with a hammer, cut somehow by a slipped wrench. He would wrap it in a handkerchief which he always kept in a pocket; then he would keep going. You had to finish the job. I remember the story of him reaching into his toolbox where a tiny rattlesnake was hiding. The snake struck him, hitting him perfectly on the nail of his thumb. Its fangs did not penetrate through the hard nail.

Clothes seemed to hang off of my father, even though in his later years he had gained a good amount of weight around his waist. There always seemed to be space in what he wore. Most often, around the farm, it was a pair of blue jeans, torn in places. He would wear work boots, generally brown or tan, with scuffs on the sides and bottom. He would spend time sitting on the brick steps leading into and out of the house, pulling and tightening the laces toward the toes, then threading the remaining laces around the eyelets leading up his ankles.

He would sigh. Great explosions of air would emerge from his lungs, generally when he was frustrated. There were a few times when I heard my father curse, but that was very rare. The sighs came when he would get up from those steps where he has laced his boots, rising to walk to the truck, to drive to the barn. As he aged, his body fought the work he did. He did not want to stop. I am not sure he could stop. It was not until his body would not do the work, that he finally did stop.

His eyes were a bright blue, but I do not remember looking into them.

His hair was blonde when he was younger. Without fanfare, it slowly moved into a light, shiny gray.

My father was so big and strong when I was a child. I felt fear in the face of his size. As he aged and as I aged, I was taller than him, eventually a good bit taller than him. I would help him to the bathroom, in and out of the car. Eventually, I would assist the nurse as we maneuvered him into the hospital bed in the hospice facility near our home.

We grow old and change. We are not the same. It is an illusion that we will always be here.

As we are told on Ash Wednesday, from dust we came and to dust we shall return.

Friday of the Third Week of Lent: Saving

To hear my father tell the story, he was afraid that he had lost me that day.

Farms are not necessarily safe places to play, but you could not tell that to a 10-year-old boy. There were gates to climb up and over. There were barns with hay bales that you could stack and climb in and around, over and through. There were pigs to chase so that you felt strong and scary. There was farm equipment that you were able to drive, sometimes.

There were also tall grain silos, those cylindrical steel canisters for storing grain or dried kernels of corn. These tall silos had ladders on the side all the way to the top, then across the slanted roof so that you could climb to the peak.

And I would.

I would scale the tall silo, rung by rung of the ladder, with that itchiness in my chest if my foot would slip a bit, peeking over the edge of the corrugated metal roof. Once at that edge, I would have to reach over and pull myself up a bit, just a bit afraid of falling back and easily twenty feet to the ground below me. But then you made it from the vertical climb to the slant of the roof. The ladder led to a circular top, a top that could be removed to allow for the circulation of air, to keep the grain dry. I would carefully sit on the tip-top of the silo, peering around at pigs, at fields, at the ways that fencing snaked along the road. I could see where my father was. I could feel a different sort of breeze from this height. And eventually, my father would call for me, and I would have to make my careful way down the roof and side of the silo.

The day he thought he lost me the silo was involved, but the danger was not falling, but "drowning".

It happened as we were harvesting corn. Those juicy ears of corn were now dry in the field, green stalks turned brown. The next step was to use a combine to move through these stalks. The stalks would fall like soldiers in front of some massive military might that was the John Deere that my father drove. The stalks would encounter the blades, be chopped off from the bottom and fall into the machine. The massive machine would separate the paper thin fiber of the plant from the cob, then pull the cob through another round of grating gears to separate the kernel of corn from the cob. The yellow kernels fell into a container sitting atop the back of the machine. The cobs and "chaff" were thrown out the bottom of the back, flying this way and that as the machine passed.

Eventually, we would pull the combine up to the back of a large truck and with the turn of a lever would move the great arm of an auger to the side and dump the contents of corn into the back of the dump truck. When it was filled, we would drive the truck full of corn back to the barn, to store in the silo.

It was great fun for me to climb to the top of the truck, to climb into the mounds of kernels of corn. They would get in your shoes, in your pockets. It was a great sea of large yellow sand in which to play. I would climb on the top and my father would drive the short distance to the silo, backing up the truck to align it with the whirling blades of another auger that would transport the seeds from the ground to the top of the silo to be stored.

After I helped my father align the truck in front of the auger, we opened a small slot at the bottom-center-back of the truck and corn flowed out of the opening, streaming like water. I climbed back into the back of the truck to play in the corn. Occasionally, my father would crank up the truck, would tilt the bed up toward the front so that more of the corn would slide toward the back. In the sea of corn in the truck, there would form a little funnel toward the back of the truck; it was fun to move closer to this whirlpool, then move away.

Yet just as a slip on the silo ladder could bring that sudden fear of falling, I felt the emptiness in my chest as I realized that I could not release my foot or my leg from the sinking corn, heading toward the silo. I am not sure whether I cried out or not. Yet I remember seeing my father above me, me up to my waist in corn, my father blotting out the sun. Despite his efforts to move the corn out from around me, it always returned, keeping me in place, with my legs moving toward the opening at the bottom of the truck, surrounded by corn up to my arms now.

Then, without sound, my father pulled me out of the place where I was caught. There were tears on my part, although I cannot say that it was because I was afraid or that I could tell how afraid my father had been. But there we both were, breathing hard, both alive together, lying flat on the shifting corn around us.

Saturday of the Third Week of Lent: Prayer

So there are parts of scripture where rain is compared to mercy and blessing. Rain was certainly something for which I remember praying in our little country church, especially during dry days of late summer.

There were four of us boys, all about eleven years old, that would hide out in the front room of the church on Sunday nights. We would stand, peering through the double doors, waiting for the time at the end of the third hymn to walk solemnly forward, down that green-carpeted middle aisle between the white-painted pews to the wooden table at the front of the church. The hymn would end, and it would be time for one of us to pray.

As for how we decided who would pray that night, sometimes we decided this in the oh-so-holy-manner of rock, paper, scissors. Other times we had a system, rotating through names, which seemed fairer. Yet no matter the method, we all took our place around that table, praying in the language of King James, thanking God for what we had been given, and praying for rain.

I think about those times of prayer as "asking" and realize that in the present, there has been a shift in my prayer life that has led me away from petitionary prayer, away from prayer where you ask God for this or that.

I have moved to much more of a sort of contemplative silence, of simply attempting to be present with God.

Other times my faith has moved from waiting on God to "fix" something to deciding to fix it myself. Maybe that is a statement of unbelief. Maybe it is a sense that God can feel quite far away at times. At my worst moments, that thought is that God is not there at all.

When someone feels gone to you, you do not ask anything else of them. You can't. They are simply not there.

In this present, my father is gone. I can no longer ask him for anything. And I am not sure that I would have for years. My mother might offer help and still does. Sometimes I accept that; sometimes I do not. But there was never a word from my father, the sort of "Remember son, I am here for you; if you need help with something, let me know." My mother would tell me that my father would do anything for me. I am not sure that I believed her. I did not ask.

At times my father had seemed weak and unable to help me, especially not in ways that I needed. As I moved into adolescence, the common areas between us grew more narrow. I was this bright, bookish kid; I do not remember him reading anything other than the Bible as I was growing up in that house.

But I do remember him complaining about the rain.

My father needed the rain. He needed it for his crops. During those dry days, my father would complain that there would be a deluge in "town", a pop-up shower over the roads and concrete. As is the case with Georgia weather in the summer, there may be a small storm in town, but not a drop of rain in the county. On our land, it was dry, stalks of corn twisting in the field.

Out of all the dry days, I can remember a handful of times when he would irrigate the crops, drawing water from the pond on the land, pouring diesel fuel into a motor that propelled water across the field.

I do not know how my father reconciled this, praying for rain and the rain remaining absent. Then, he would take the matter into his own hands. For me, as a young boy at the front of that little country church, it did not feel that my prayer made much difference either.

Yet we prayed for rain.

Now as I think about this act, this praying for rain, it seems like a sort of thinking that if I pray in the right way then God will reward my prayer. It is a sort of thinking that is much less about mercy and grace and more about control, ultimately our control, not God's control.

So it would rain in town that day. My father would read his Bible that night in the kitchen at the bar where we took most of our meals. He would mumble his prayers in a way that I could not hear him if I had wanted to. Then he would go to bed.

And sometimes it would rain.

Fourth Sunday of Lent: Raising up our Hurt

One of the readings for this Sunday is the raising of the staff with the serpent from Numbers 21. It is an old story of the people grumbling.

If you unfamiliar, there are a host of tales of the people of Israel leaving Egypt, where they had been enslaved. But as they follow this God and this man Moses from oppression into freedom, this freedom looks frightening. The way is hard; it is challenging. The people are walking through the Red Sea. They are wandering through the wilderness. They are eating only the food that God is providing for them, this manna, for days and days, then weeks, then years.

"Why have you brought us out of Egypt to die here?" they ask, over and over. And while it may be easy for us to say, "Just trust God," I think I would have grumbled too.

In this story, God becomes so weary of the grumbling that poisonous snakes appear among the people to bite them. Without qualms about the nature of a God who would do such a thing, the story simply states that many people died. The people who survive go to Moses to ask him to intercede with God on their behalf, to take the snakes away from them.

But God does not take the snakes away.

God instead has Moses create a snake made of bronze. Moses attaches it to a pole and then raises this snake high above the people so that those who have been bitten can look on this bronze snake and then be healed, a strange cure to be certain.

The cure is that we must look at what hurt us in order to live.

I am a therapist, a clinical social worker by training. There are many with whom I have sat that know that when they come to me, we will look at what hurt. Most of these wounds are emotional and mental, although that often comes with physical injury as well. Our wounds carry pain; they burn as the venom continues to work its way through our system, infecting our thoughts about ourselves and our thoughts about others. Over time this venom infects our biology in ways affects us physically, not just mentally, although the mental pain is enough.

So we raise up what hurt us. We look at it long and hard, seeing it clearly so that it cannot hurt us anymore.

On this particular Sunday in the season of Lent, this passage about the snakes is paired with the story of Nicodemus going to Jesus, by night.

Nicodemus had to go by night because he was a religious leader in that community; to be seen with Jesus during the day would have possibly cost him his position. He wanted to talk to Jesus about being "born again" or depending on your translation, "born from above".

Nicodemus struggles with these teachings of Jesus. He struggles with who Jesus says that he is. And in the context of this conversation, Jesus says that Jesus too will be lifted up just as Moses lifted up the serpent in the wilderness.

We will have to look at our hurt, the hurt we have caused and the hurt that has been done to us. We will have to have it raised over our heads and fully see it.

This is the path to rebirth. This is the way.

Monday of the Fourth Week of Lent: Darker

It is darker this morning.

For reasons that many will debate in this country, we "spring forward" around this time of year, moving our clocks from 2 am to 3 am early Sunday morning, losing an hour of sleep, ostensibly so that there will be an additional hour of daylight in the evening. The net effect for us early-risers is that the sunrise is now an hour away.

For years now, I have arisen early in the mornings to run, to have the quiet of that time. Thomas Merton once commented about how meditation was like that. Prayer does not make the sun rise but ensures that one will be awake for it.

But now, around the anniversary of my father's death, even with the distance of years, I feel this time as simply dark. It is harder to get up and out of bed.

There are ways that we begin to feel like light and life are returning when we are in the midst of grief. Those moments of brief joy return. You laugh a bit easier. You appreciate something silly that a child does instead of feeling annoyed by it.

But then the wave returns; the light is now further away. The pain feels closer today.

As a child, I remember crying about going to the farm. Often I did not want to go because there was not much for me to do. Other times I did not want to do the task that my father wanted me to do. Inevitably I would not do it well enough, would face his disapproval, would hear "if you want it done right, you have to do it yourself" except this time it was directed at me. He would go behind me, fixing what I had broken, completing what I had left unfinished.

There were times and tasks that did require my hands, even my limited boyish strength. Some of these were necessary but ugly jobs. Often this involved me getting the piglets, these young, squealing, scared pigs out of the faring house.

The faring house consisted of an aisle in the center with nine pens, four on one side and five on the other, with the pens raised off of the floor about a foot on cement blocks. We would move the sows into their pen as they were getting closer to giving birth. The pen was just barely big enough for the pregnant sow, about six feet square. When the sow gave birth, we would pull gates closer around them, placing them diagonally in the square. This was to keep them from laying on their newly born piglets. The sow had just enough room to stand, then to lie on her side so that the piglets could nurse.

So as a young boy, my job was to climb the side of the pen and reach over the grab the piglets, being careful to stay out of reach of the sow. I would hand the wriggling, squealing piglet to my father who would then give them some sort of medicine, then return them to the pen with their mother. These tiny pigs would release a high-pitched squeal, kicking and fighting, out of the pen, to my father, then back again.

There came a time too as the pigs matured that we had to "break their tusks". Again this meant getting them out of the pen with their mother, handing them to my father, except this time I had to help him hold the pig to keep it from squirming and freeing itself. We would hold their head still while my father would reach into the piglets screaming mouth with a pair of pliers. He would place the pliers around one of the emerging tusks, holding it hard then turn his strong wrist to the side, cracking and breaking the forming tusk from the piglet's mouth. He would do one side then the other. Then, as before, I would return the screaming piglet to its mother.

Weeks later we would return again to castrate the male piglets.

The piglets were older at this point, bigger, harder to hold on to, and at this point were separated from their mother in another pen on a concrete slab, with a partial shelter and a feeding trough.

As before, I would catch the males, struggle to hold them and bring them to my father. He held a single razor blade. As I placed a knee on the pig to hold it in place, my father would squeeze the scrotum of the piglet, make a quick cut in the sack, force out the testicles, and cut the cord that attached them. In an additional quick motion, he would toss the testicles off to the side, telling me to release the pig. I did, and the pig would run away from us, squealing, bleeding.

It is no wonder to me now that I did not like going down to the barn and that I would cry about having to do these tasks.

Yet now as an adult, I recognize that there is a brutality to living and working that is unavoidable. We can try to make it quaint and sanitary, but there are piss and shit, blood and screaming. And there is death.

Tuesday of the Fourth Week of Lent: Fault

Was it my fault? Whose fault was it? Who is responsible? Why was this person born blind? We look for a reason for something being different, especially when we equate that difference with some sort of suffering, lack, or injury.

There is an innate need that all of us have for some sort of predictability and control. One researcher that I have read regarding the effects of long-term stress on our health writes eloquently about how our human brains do a much better job of looking ahead, of planning, of weighing options. This is an advantage for the most part, except that we often assume much more control than actually exists.

Then when something does go wrong, we get angry and blame others. Or we get sad and blame ourselves. Or we get anxious and worry about when the bad event is going to happen again.

In theological terms, we tend to talk about "sin". And in the portion of John that I read this morning, there is this debate among the disciples with Jesus about a man who was born blind.

The disciples ask, "Rabbi (teacher), who sinned that this man was born blind? Did he sin or did his parents?" And Jesus responds, "Neither. He was born blind so that God's works might be revealed in him."

Personally, I am not sure that I am entirely satisfied with that answer. Yet, it is a dramatic improvement over either blaming this man who is blind or blaming the blind man's parents. What is probably more telling is that Jesus does not spend his time debating whether God punishes people by making them blind or not; Jesus moves to heal the man.

He spits in the dirt, makes mud, and rubs the mud on the man's eyes. He then instructs him to go and wash in a nearby pool.

As is often the case, Jesus acts with compassion, not condemnation, an action that involved spit and dirt, that was physical and real.

Physical and real and hard is how I would describe the work that my father and I did on the farm. I can still feel in my body what it was like to run after the hogs, trying to guide them into another pen, or up a chute onto a truck so that they could be taken to be sold. I can feel the weight of a bag of soybeans, to open it, to feel the seed inside the bag, to lift it up and pour the seed into the hopper on the planter. The smell of diesel fumes permeated the air around the tractor as my father would pull away from the truck where I sat.

There were few words exchanged. The words that my father did say were about what to hand him, what to do next, and what I might have done wrong. If I had only run a bit harder in the other direction then the hog would not have gotten away from us. Then we would not have had to chase it one more time.

And it is no wonder how we as children begin to overestimate our control of the world. We are taught this story from our parents: work hard and you will succeed. Do the right thing; it will work out best. Don't "sin", and God will always favor you.

But then the longer you live, the more you realize that this is an illusion. And that the control you thought you had by "doing the right thing", by not "sinning", is illusory. It is an idol. There is a sneaky way that this sense of control makes you a god.

Sometimes people are just born blind.

Thursday of the Fourth Week of Lent: Both

We moved our family because of new life . . . and because of approaching death.

The timing of Easter depends on the last full moon of the vernal equinox. This gleaming object in the dark of night tells us when we can release ourselves from Lent, moving through the dark days of Good Friday and Holy Saturday to the new life of Easter. There is darkness, and there is a new light. Images of paradox inhabit this faith. This is also part of the way.

As my wife and I, we left our positions as clergy along the coast of Georgia in the name of the new lives that had joined us and in the approaching death of my father.

My father was diagnosed with idiopathic pulmonary fibrosis a year prior to our move. During that year, my wife and I brought two children into our home, one by birth and the other by adoption.

We had been frenetically engaged in an adoption process that would eventually bring home our daughter. That process involved background checks and fingerprints, homestudies and social workers. While many pregnancies "just happen", the paper pregnancy that we were nurturing along required work, notaries, and travel to immigration services.

As we went through the checklist of tasks associated with the adoption, there were also trips to my hometown to take my father to a pulmonologist, for him to sit in an enclosed plastic tube to gauge lung functioning. These were checklists that looked at criteria for a diagnosis. When we finally received the diagnosis of IPF, the physician told us the diagnosis was terminal, with a typical prognosis of one to two years.

My hospice experience told me that my father would have a long and slow demise, becoming "bedbound and dependent for all ADLs". This meant that he would become less able to care for himself, eventually confined to a hospital bed, rails up on the sides, where he would be fed, bathed, and toileted.

At the same time, my wife was now pregnant with our son as we waited for a travel date for our daughter. We were putting together cribs (beds with rails) and infant toys, receiving gifts of bottles, and diapers and wipes. The ends of our lives look astonishing like the beginning, with someone taking care of our most basic needs: feeding, bathing, toileting.

There is a symmetry to birth and death. We found ourselves anticipating both.

Lent itself is full of these conflicting images. There are images of denial and withdrawal at the same time when we see new leaves and new life springing from the ground. We move toward Good Friday, a reminder of a horrible death, yet looking for a way to new life.

Friday of the
Fourth Week of Lent:
Idols

"You know your father is one of the best men I have ever met," he said.

At the time I heard this, I lived in that in-between place of dorms or apartments, returning home on some weekends here and there, intermittently in the summers, going away again to school in the fall.

The timing for these words was early spring. I was home briefly and had been instructed to go down to the accountant's office to sign a tax return. As I sat in front of the accountant's desk, in a wood-paneled office, I saw a man that had guided my father through many years of self-employment as a farmer.

"He is one of the best men I have ever met," he said.

As my father aged, there was less to do on the farm. Eventually, he sold his last truckful of hogs, even the sows! He began to sell equipment, to tear down old barns and fencing. The tall metal grain silo was sold for scrap metal. The farm that I knew as a boy was being slowly and steadily dismantled.

And as this accountant went on and on about my father, I felt a dismantling of the image that I had of my father. Through another's eyes, I was seeing him anew. My eyes viewed my father through the struggle of being his son. These eyes saw my father as a man who had lived and worked in this community for over fifty years. My father was a man who stuck to his word, that knew that your name means something.

His name did mean something.

In my own experience as a son who has lost a father, and in my work as a counselor with many sons who have lost fathers, the death of the father for a son is an event that brings a time of questioning and reconsideration, a dismantling of a sort. No matter what kind of father is now gone, we feel a space where they lived in us. This loss is one that we feel emotionally, theologically, and psychologically.

Sigmund Freud, the father of modern psychology and himself an atheist, theorized in The Future of an Illusion (1928) that we project our idealized father outside of us, that we manufacture a deity based on this projection. Therefore this "Father God" to whom many pray is who we wish our own fathers to be, a fantasized form, an ideal father in the image of God.

And perhaps there is some truth there; I have met many men and women for whom their relationship with their father has clearly affected how they view God and their faith, especially in an environment dominated by a branch of Christianity that prizes the image of God as father.

Hopefully, this projected/idealized image is not who God remains for us. According to one writer, this God as projected father was not the end for Freud either.

Mark Edmundson posits that at the end of Freud's life, in Freud's last published work Moses and Monotheism (1939), that the psychoanalyst began to see the value in his own Jewish heritage, a heritage that included the revolutionary insight of denying the idol (or idols).

In Judaism, there was to be no "graven image" of God. It is in this way, by denying any physical representation of God, that God moved inside of us. We were not constantly trying to encounter a being outside, but instead, we would be plumbing the depths of ourselves, allowing a non-represented, non-imaged God to be open and elusive.

God was not out there; God was in us.

Perhaps this too is the way that our fathers are at first outside of us, instructing us, telling us the difference between a flathead and a Phillips-head screwdriver. This father is "larger than life" but slowly shrinks as we grow. And then one day, eventually, they leave us.

And that leaving is initially felt like a loss, an absence. But then we hear their voice in our voice, sometimes saying the same sort of phrases that we heard our own father's say. We notice ourselves looking like them, acting as they did, even thinking thoughts that you are sure that they thought too.

The leaving is not an absence, but a transformation.

Saturday of the
Fourth Week of Lent:
Space

It is when time slows, when the busyness of the week is over, when there is openness in the day, that grief rushes in to fill that space.

For me, this is especially true of these Saturdays during the time of Lent. If every Sunday is a "little resurrection" during this time, then every Saturday is a time to mourn the death, to be confused at what has happened, to not know what to do next.

As we read in the gospels, we can imagine the disciples on that Saturday after Jesus's death not understanding what had happened. After all, there was the hope for a new king, a savior. In our limited vision, we imagine this "saving" being done in a way that we can see and touch. We all can be guilty of having this sort of limited vision of who Jesus is, mostly based on who we want him to be.

Yet what had just happened in front of the disciples was a death, a horrible, ignoble death.

And now there is the space of the day after.

In the days after my father's death, I tell a story that many who have grieved will tell. There are conversations that I do not remember. There are meals that I picked at and ate. There is moving through my days as if I were moving through a fog, a thickness to the air, a weight to my movement. Sometimes I kept myself busy, filling that emptiness. Sometimes loss overwhelmed me.

There is a danger in that time, in that space after death. As much as the disciples felt a danger to being identified as a follower of Jesus, there is a felt danger to being in this in-between place of grieving. People are uncomfortable with you being there. They often do not know what to say other than, "I'm sorry for your loss." There is pressure, sometimes subtle, sometimes more overt, to "move on".

There is a truth that one does not want to settle into this in-between place, this wilderness of grief. Yet I do believe that this wandering is longer for some, due to the nature of the relationship lost, due to the complications of that loss.

Ideally, we are moving from death to some sort of new place, through the changes that come with loss, to a new life.

There is Christian mystic Marguerite Porete who writes about moving beyond the "law" to the law of love, moving from the little church to the "big" church.

For Porete, the ultimate goal was union with the Divine through love. For her, this necessitated a giving up of everything except knowing the love of God. This is a giving up of our attachments, physical and mental, to know only God through love, to unite our will to that love.

In some ways that is what I imagine happens in this in-between place, but again the in-between is a place that feels empty. Struggle and danger are there. It is a place where we face our loss, the loss of the other, even the loss of ourselves.

John of the Cross writes this another way: "The soul that is attached to anything, however much good there may be in it, will not arrive at the liberty of divine union. For whether it be a strong wire rope or a slender and delicate thread that holds the bird, it matters not, if it really holds it fast; for until the cord be broken the bird cannot fly."

In our grief, we feel broken, unmoored, untethered. Yet maybe in that space, there is also a freedom to fly.

Fifth Sunday of Lent: Decay

Robert Frost writes, "The same leaves over and over again! They fall from giving shade above, To make one texture of faded brown, And fit the earth like a leather glove. Before the leaves can mount again, To fill the trees with another shade, They must go down past things coming up. They must go down into the dark decayed."

This time of Lent is very much about penitence, about honesty, about identifying where there is "sin" or hurt or brokenness. This is an austere time, yet there is the contrast of budding leaves on trees. Flowers burst forth from bulbs hidden underneath the ground. The ground has been warmed by the sun, moistened by the rain, taking the fallen leaves from before and making them into nourishment for new life.

The new life seems hidden for a while during the gathering darkness of winter, then slowly, it emerges.

Yesterday was another visit to Dublin, to the place where I was raised, to the land in which I was planted and sprouted and grew. I noticed sprigs of fresh green leaves emerging from fields near our home. As I drove by other fields there were clean lines of freshly turned and planted soil, deep red and brown lines all the way to the woods. There is a smell that comes with that moist soil. I felt myself taking deep draws of air into my lungs.

Yesterday was also a visit with a friend. We turned over the soil of our lives, allowing some of the what had been difficult to rest there, to be turned over, to move deeper into the soil and become nutrients for what would blossom the next spring. We both told difficult stories from our past, seeing ways that good had eventually emerged.

The leaves fell and eventually decayed. New leaves came the next year.

This time is different in my life. My father is gone. He was here for many seasons, and then he fell too. I see in myself and in my friend the way that we display the seasons through which we have traveled, through which we are still traveling.

He talked about seeing people in our hometown recently, people he had not seen in a long while. "They all look old," he laughed.

And I thought that we did too.

Lent, this period of preparation for Easter, travels through the darkness of Good Friday, of Holy Saturday. There does not seem to be another way, except an honest journey through the hurt, the "sin", and the brokenness.

Tuesday of the Fifth Week of Lent: Arguing

"I can't talk as good as you can."

My father said this to me as early as ten or eleven. These words came when he wanted me to call an office for him, to make an appointment or some other official business. Then he would say, "You know I'm just a poor old farmer."

And while there is something alluring about being asked to behave like an adult when one is still a child, it was also nervous-making. When I have talked with people who have been in similar situations with their parents, I have used the image of a child wearing a parent's coat. One may feel a bit more grown-up in wearing it, but the garment is ill-fitting, loose, uncomfortable.

"Why do I have to?!?" I would argue.

"I'm just a poor old farmer. I don't know how to talk to them like you do."

Children, obey your parents, I could hear in my head.

Another voice throughout Lent is a story of liberation. It is the liberation of the people from sin. As the coming story of Holy Week proclaims, these events happened during the celebration of Passover, a Jewish celebration to commemorate the liberation of the children of Israel from slavery in Egypt, of Moses leading them to the promised land.

But at the beginning of that story, Moses did not want to speak either.

Moses's claimed that he had a problem with his speech. According to Jewish scholar Avivah Zornberg, this same word that Moses used for his tongue, that it was "heavy", is the same Hebrew word used for Pharaoh's heart, that it was also "heavy" or "resistant" or "closed off".

In her research through the Midrashic tradition, Zornberg believes that Moses needed convincing that God would be present with him, just as much as the people would also need to be convinced. On first glance, it seems that Moses is arguing about his ability to speak, but perhaps Moses was not confident in the message.

Moses's arguing with God was about needing to believe.

Sometimes we all argue with God because of our need to believe.

As for me, I remember arguing with my father at these moments about a phone call, a time when I was being asked to speak, but did not feel confident in what I was saying. Part of me needed to see my father as strong, capable, and able to handle himself in the world.

Yet, there were many times when he was not. He was anxious and afraid, not feeling sure of himself enough to call to make an appointment at a doctor's office. I didn't want to call either, but then I was a child. Yet I pressed my finger to the numbers on the rotary phone, spinning the dial to the left, digit by digit, click click click click click, my fingers feeling heavy and slow as I dialed.

"Hello? May I speak to . . .

Wednesday of the Fifth Week of Lent: Fire

There were cycles to days on the farm.

Most days began with feeding the hogs in the morning and checking on the sows and piglets. This was generally my father's job. During the summer and on school breaks, the next step would be climbing into a 1984 blue and white Ford and taking a slow drive to Huddle House for breakfast, where I would eat a cheese danish while reading a book. He would drink coffee and talk with the other older men.

If there was business "in town", we would handle it then. This business may be filling a drum with diesel fuel while talking with Mr. J.B. Burch, buying some seed and more talking with someone at Roche, and occasionally stopping by an old gas station where my father would sit and talk with "Cook".

There was a lot of talking involved in farming; for me, there was a lot of reading.

Eventually, we would return home, change clothes, and begin some task around the farm until lunch. Lunch was generally a sandwich while my father watched *The Young and the Restless*. After, we would be a return to the farm, to plant or to harvest. The pigs would be tended to again toward the end of the day. Depending on when the sun would set would determine the end of the day of work.

There were cycles to the year as well. While the peanuts grew, we would walk the rows and pull pigweeds, these spiny stalks with spiny leaves that would grow in between the peanut plants. You had to learn how to grab them just right, to pull, to not get "stuck" by those prickly stalks. There was something satisfying about pulling them from the rich soil, the smell that emerged and laying them to the side.

Crops grew in their own cycles as well. The corn would grow high in the summer, and plentiful enough that you could lose myself in the rows. The wheat was planted and grew through the spring into early summer. I remember putting those small grains in my mouth, chewing them, tasting raw flour. After that harvest, there was the burning of the field of wheat stalks, those dry stalks left following the harvest.

For a young boy, it was exciting to be around that much fire. The flames themselves were minimal, slowly creeping, catching stalk by stalk. The real danger was the heat and smoke ahead of the flames.

As a young boy steeped in the Bible as taught by my Aunt Francis in Sunday School, I knew the story of Shadrach, Meshach, and Abednego. This was the story of the fiery furnace, of these three who had been thrown into that fiery furnace by a king who would not tolerate disobedience. These three had said that they would not worship an image constructed by the king. And for that crime, they were to be killed.

So into a roaring fire, they were thrown.

Yet in the midst of the flames, they lived. These three marched around with a fourth person that "had the appearance of a god". And as I marched around those tiny flames burning the stalks of wheat, I imagined being in the midst of those flames. But these flames were not simply to destroy, but to burn away what was no longer needed, to prepare the field for what was to come. This was fire as purifying force.

The cycle of Lent, this season of Lent, contains images of purification too. We begin with the image of ashes, the remains of the burned palms from Palm Sunday the year prior. On Ash Wednesday we hear "You are dust and to dust, you shall return". This is not merely an image of destruction, but renewal and purification. There remains much in our lives that needs to be burned away, purified in some sense.

What is being burned away may have been important, useful; the stalk that lifted the grain of wheat into the air gave it support and nourishment. While the stalk was important for a time, the cycle is now complete. It is time to burn away what is no longer needed.

As we walk through this purification that is Lent, may we hold to what is true, much like Shadrach, Meshach, and Abednego, but may we also be willing to allow some of who we are, some of who we think God is, to be purified, to burn and be lifted away, as a pleasing incense to this God.

Friday of the Fifth Week of Lent: Bitter Herbs

This is a world in which it is easy to become numb, to anesthetize ourselves.

The anesthesia says, "It will never change. This is just how people are. There is nothing that I can do."

We are bombarded with images on our screens of tragedy, of shootings and bombings, of political dysfunction, of people demonizing each other instead of finding a common humanity.

It is tempting to throw up our hands, to walk away, to numb ourselves again. Yet, we are called to walk *through* the difficulty, not to avoid the pain. We cannot avoid the hard work of these problems.

We have to eat the bitter herbs, together.

As we move through this season of Lent, toward this Holy Week, there is the congruence with Passover, the Jewish remembrance of the events of the Exodus. Jesus celebrated this Passover meal with the disciples, a meal that remembers the history of slavery, a meal that precedes liberation.

In that meal there are many elements: lamb, an egg, a vegetable dipped in salty water, all symbolic of the struggle of that passage from slavery to freedom. And on that traditional plate are bitter herbs. These herbs serve as a remembrance but also as a participation in the bitterness of the time of being enslaved.

We remember by participating. We remember by being present with suffering.

As a therapist, there are times you often find yourself *feeling with* the other person in front of you. People come into my office to tell their story. These may be stories of grief or abuse, of the trauma of an event as dramatic as war or the sort of trauma that some of us experience as our childhood.

And we tell the story again, and again, and again.

Stories are told as a series of events, but then also as a succession of feelings. There are feelings of desperation or fear, sadness and sorrow. Sometimes in the midst of the stories, there are tears.

To be honest, there are times when I feel those tears well up in my own eyes just as they do in the person sitting across from me at that moment. There are times when you can only cry *with* the person sitting in front of you, not fixing the hurt, but being present with the hurt.

In that time and space, we are sitting there together, client and clinician, therapist and patient. In reality, we are just two people.

Together, we are remembering a time that was past, a hurt that had happened "back then", but there is also a strange sort of participation in the present. In that office, in that space, we remember the event; we also participate in it again, even if that means crying again. And in the end, we hope for healing . . . and resurrection.

As a person of faith, this is a time of the year where I anticipate the cycle of Holy Week. Holy Week consists of a remembering/re-participation in Maundy Thursday, Good Friday, the desolation of Holy Saturday, and eventually Easter. We walk again through the events of Jesus's triumphant entry into Jerusalem, his trial and death, the emptiness of that Saturday in between, and finally the emptiness of the tomb.

There is the temptation to run roughshod over the days in between. But we must remember that a part of our faith, a part of our lives, are those difficult days in between.

We must eat the bitter herbs.

Walter Brueggemann writes that he sees the crucifixion of Jesus as "the ultimate act of prophetic criticism" because of the participation *in* death. He writes that Jesus one where God "embraces the death that people must die". Brueggemann sees this death as a participation, a full incarnation, an act of "passion and compassion that completely and irresistibly undermine the world of competence and competition. The contrast is stark and total: this passionate man set in the midst of numbed Jerusalem. And only the passion can finally penetrate the numbness."

In eating the bitter herbs we stand with those places in our lives that remain bitter and difficult. In walking through this holy week, we remember the pain of those who die without cause, those who were innocent. We fight against a numbness that tells us that we cannot change this world, that we cannot help, that we cannot raise our voices for change.

We can say, "This is enough."

Sixth Sunday of Lent: Palms and Passion

This is a strange Sunday. It is a strange Sunday because we begin with a parade of a sort. Jesus is entering Jerusalem. He tells the disciples to "borrow" a colt, on which Jesus will sit as he rides into town. From the people, there are shouts of hosanna and "Blessed is the one who comes in the name of the Lord!" while the people lay out cloaks and branches to prepare the way of this king. This is how Palm Sunday begins.

This is also the way that many of us begin . . . with hopes and dreams, sometimes ones that can be a bit far-fetched. As a therapist who works with children I sometimes ask them, "What do you think you might want to be when you grow up?" The younger ones answer with things like race car driver or astronaut or a famous sports player. As they get older, the adolescents begin to answer this same question in a much more "realistic" way.

And this is part of what is happening in this passage. Scholars mostly agree that as Jesus enters the city, these people shouting "Hosanna" were looking for a political savior. The people were hoping and praying for change from the oppressive Roman rule under which they lived. They were looking for liberation. And something about this Jesus of Nazareth signaled to them that this might be it. This one who rode on a colt, as humble as this gesture would be, this one would be the one who saves us, all of us . . . finally.

Of course, riding on a colt was not the same as a powerful warhorse. And this battle was not one of military might. Instead, this redemption would follow the path through death to new life. This change would come, but the walk is not one of continual triumph.

On this Sunday, this strange Sunday, we celebrate with the palms, then we move to remember the passion. Once more we hear this story of Jesus being brought to trial, accused by the religious leaders of that day, questioned by Pilate. And Pilate asks Jesus, "Have you no answer?"

The text reads that Pilate was amazed by the silence.

Jesus was silent . . . quiet . . . and did not respond.

Part of what this passion means to us is that the call to follow Jesus is not one that leads to power in the way that the world knows power. Following this Jesus means that sometimes we will not have an answer that satisfies the world and the way that the world sees power.

Sometimes the only answer we have is the cross.

Our answer has to do with suffering with those who are hurting. Our answer is not one of retaliation; we do not answer violence with more violence. We are called to be with those who are hurting, having compassion and love for them. Even though he was greeted like a king, Jesus empties himself for us, walks with us, even unto his death.

This is the way that leads to resurrection.

So, today we read the story of the palms; we also read the story of the passion. We take these words with us into this Holy Week, living with this text, being with this story. Walk with this story, walking the way of peace, even through the valley of the shadow of death, knowing that God is with you, that God is bringing new life out of death, out of tragedy.

Monday of the Sixth Week of Lent: Cleansing

Spring is time for cleaning. And although it has lost much spiritual significance, there is a historically *spiritual* reason for the cleaning.

This time of Lent was a preparation of the new converts to be brought into the community of faith. They were preparing themselves, spiritually, for baptism, for the way in which all Christians are received into the church. But as time went on, there was a group participation in this Lent, this preparation. The whole community moved through these rituals of a meal (Maundy Thursday), a death (Good Friday), the time in between, and the dawning of new life (Easter).

The first Easter after my father's death did not feel like much of a celebration. I still walked through the fog that comes with grief, not feeling present in the world. There were times when the reality of his death would come again, emerging from the mist, shocking me again. There remained the struggle with who he had been in my life, what sort of father he was. There was the anxiety that emerges with the questions of what would happen next, to me, to my mother, and to the land on which I had been raised.

The land looked different than it did when I grew up there.

Much of the "cleaning" of the farm was done before his death, by my father alone. He cleared the land over the course of years, while I was away at college, then in graduate school in Virginia, and eventually back to Georgia.

My father dismantled much of the rickety fence that formerly contained sows and piglets, feeder pigs, and hogs ready to take to the market. There were wooden planks to tear apart. There was a man who came by, offering to tear down an old barn for my father as long as he could keep the wood. Somewhere, some stranger's mantle over a fireplace is made of wood that was an old hay barn on our property.

I wonder what it was like for my father, walking along the fence that he had repaired over and over. This time he was tearing the fence apart, rolling up old wire, placing old boards one-by-one on a pile. My father was an old man, having worked on this land since he was five years old, to hear him tell it. Working hard was all that he knew. When he reached a point where his knee would not allow him to climb up and down off of a John Deere tractor, I believed that he would not live much longer.

He did live on after the clearing of the land, but he was miserable.

What do any of us do when our meaning has left us? What do any of us do when our purpose changes, disappears, or is by necessity removed?

How must it have felt for him to have been the one to take the old farm apart, board by board?

As we begin this Holy Week, there were traditions of cleansing, of cleaning the church ahead of this week in preparation for Easter. I have noticed many churches around me making final preparations to their landscaping, refreshing the mulch or pine straw, planting new spring flowers. This preparation is to welcome those who arrive on Sunday.

Yet the true preparation happens internally, within us.

There are fences inside us that need to be taken apart. And although those fences gave definition to the land, a set of lines to live by, there are times when we have to remove them. Sometimes these are old notions about who God is, that while these ideas are important for a season in our lives, that there is a time to allow God to be larger than our idea of who God should be.

And yes, sometimes it is our job to walk along that old fence, remembering it, honoring what it did, but then taking it apart . . . board by board.

Tuesday of the Sixth Week of Lent: Meaning

I did not always understand what my father meant by what he said.

There were phrases that he used, such as "hot-aw-mighty-nose", or at least that is what it sounded like to me as a child. For the longest time, I thought that this particular utterance had something to do with high temperatures and your sense of smell! It was after years that I figured out that this curse was him saying "God almighty knows!"

But even in my confusion, I did not ask. Now that may have been in part because he was cursing; I may have been afraid that it was something that I had done or would get directed at me next. Regardless of the reason, I never asked: "what does that mean?"

Although nearly all of my memories of my father are connected to the farm, farming was a second try for my father.

The first effort had been in conjunction with my Uncle Edsel, the entrepreneur in the family. Together they owned the Allis-Chalmers tractor dealership in town. As I understand the arrangement, my uncle was a consummate salesman. My father was a mechanic. And while my uncle was selling tractors, hay balers, and cotton pickers, my father would be traveling over several counties, working in fields to fix what had broken.

My father was the one they called to help them try again.

This is where my father built his strong arms. The bulk of his arms came from turning wrenches and manipulating heavy steal. Meanwhile, my uncle sat inside the dealership, working with the money and paper. If you stood them side-by-side you could see the difference in their physiques.

In this time as I travel through middle age, one of my regrets is that I did not learn much from him regarding the mechanics of tractors and combines, hay balers, and cotton pickers. My father was determined as he worked. I felt scared to ask "why" we were placing grease in a certain joint. I had to keep fumbling around in the toolbox to find the etched writing that told me the size of the wrench; my father would know the size of the wrench by sight, maybe even by touch. He just knew.

I never got the chance to ask him, "What does this mean?"

Where this question, "What does this mean?" is given voice, is in the instructions regarding Passover.

There is a strong connection in meaning between Passover and Lent. Readings overlap with Exodus telling us about the deliverance of the people of Israel from slavery; the readings from the gospels and Paul are about deliverance from sin and death.

In Exodus 13:14, there is an explicit reference to the question of a child to a parent. "What does this mean?" the child asks. The question comes after there are explicit instructions about how to prepare the lamb for Passover. The instructions come in preparation for leaving Egypt, fleeing slavery.

The answer that the parent is supposed to give the child is this: "By strength of hand the Lord brought us out of Egypt, from the house of slavery."

We do look for strength in those who lead us, although how we define that strength varies wildly, whether that is a strength of hand or intellect. We do not wish to follow those who seem weak. We do not trust someone who cannot protect us, who seems unable to fight for themselves. We know that the road to liberation is difficult.

In the Passover narrative, this path would involve the killing of a lamb, the eating of bitter herbs, the making of quick bread because there was little time to wait. This path can be difficult and bloody.

So when we ask "What does it all mean?" this is what we are told to say: "By strength of hand the Lord brought us out of Egypt . . .".

The Allis-Chalmers dealership failed. And what my father had left was a tractor, the family land, and a pair of strong arms.

There are times when we search for meaning, trying to appeal to the intellect, to try to understand our faith or what God is doing. Sometimes meaning will fail or be difficult to understand.

There are other moments where we place our hand in another strong hand, to help us along the way, to liberation.

Wednesday of the Sixth Week of Lent: Spy

Wallace Shawn writes, "The perfectly decent person who follows a certain chain of reasoning, ever so slightly and subtly incorrect, becomes a perfect monster at the end of the chain."

There is a theory that Judas knew what he was doing.

The theory runs that this one who betrayed Jesus into the hands of the authorities was part of a group who was looking for a *political* savior. Judas thought Jesus was this sort of savior or Messiah. The theory is that Judas thought that if Jesus was to confront the authorities, that Jesus would by necessity fight.

This was not unreasonable . . . as is most of our thinking, about this Jesus, about God. And as Shawn writes, we can all be perfectly decent people whose ever so slightly twisted logic makes us monsters at the end.

In therapy circles, we sometimes talk about "cognitive distortions", ways of thinking that color how we view the world. One example that I frequently use is how peering through a blue lens tints the world we see blue. These distortions are born out of our experiences, especially those that happened when we were young.

This day of Holy Week is sometimes called "Spy Wednesday" because of a tradition that says that Judas had made his deal this day. It is the day ahead of Maundy Thursday when Jesus would celebrate the Passover with his disciples. After this meal, which Christians now celebrate as the Lord's Supper, the authorities would arrest Jesus, try him, and crucify him on Friday.

But it is this day that makes me wonder where *our* distortions lie? What is the "slightly incorrect logic followed to the end" that turns any of us from decent people into monsters?

An important part of our Jewish heritage is the lack of an image of God. In that tradition, even the name of God was written *without* vowels. There was an openness, a lack of definition as to who God was. And while for some this presents an uncomfortable ambiguity, it also keeps us from making God in *our own image*. This lack of definition guards against our own distortions.

Remember that spies whisper to us. They encourage us to believe distortions about others, about ourselves, and even about our God.

Maundy Thursday

We did not talk much on the trips back and forth to the bathroom.

These trips happened at several treatment facilities, even in a hotel. Toileting is a basic necessity that with my father's arthritis and growing weakness from chemotherapy and radiation had become increasingly difficult.

He would thank me, make some comment about me taking care of "this old man". I commented a couple of times that he had taken care of me, as I helped him out of the bathroom stall, into the chair, over to the sink to wash his hands.

There was a reciprocity to this action, an equaling, an evening.

On Maundy Thursday, in many churches, there is often a foot-washing. This tradition comes from the actions by Jesus on this night, following the celebration of the Passover, this first Lord's Supper.

Jesus gives them a *new commandment*. This is where the name of this day emerges. Maundy comes to us from the Latin *mandatum*, meaning "commandment". This new commandment was to "love one another". This love was not shown in words, but in Jesus, the teacher, this Son of God, washing their feet.

The commandment is for them to do for others as Jesus had done for them, to empty themselves, to give, to love.

It is a strange thing to me that as modern Christians there is a drive to power and success, often measured in numbers like attendance or money. Yet this was never a concern to Jesus, who disrobed and washed his own disciples' feet.

This Maundy Thursday was a day when those who were called "the penitents", those seeking forgiveness and reconciliation with God and with the community of faith are welcomed again.

For me, these actions, of humbling, of penitence, of asking forgiveness and receiving reconciliation, these themes move together. This is the path.

I feel a sort of reconciliation with my father. I see him for who he was, with his own hurts and sorrows, fears and sadness. He also had a wink and a smile that let you know that there were joy and humor there too.

I see him in me. I hope that I honor him with who I have become, even when I too feel that I have failed and am in need of forgiveness.

Maybe some of the words of gratitude are mumbled, back and forth. Yet the words are true. Maybe the words are not what is most important, but the guiding of a wheelchair, the opening of a door, the assistance with a most basic function, then the slow return to the waiting room.

There is a sacrament, there is a holiness there too.

Good Friday

My father spent two weeks in an inpatient hospice facility, about two miles from the land he farmed. His physician had told him that they were checking him into the facility to "build him up" again. I do not know whether my father believed this or not.

The design of the space had a large common area, with flowers, a television, multiple sofas and coffee tables. There was a small dining area toward the back. All of the rooms connected to this one room. The common area was a sort of center, a "still point" that all radiated out from.

My father's room was sparse, clinical. The TV stand, the nightstand, the bed, the chair/recliner all rested on wheels. The floors were cold, industrial tile. All of this makes the room functional, easy to clean. As we checked my father into the facility, we stripped him of the clothing that I remember him wearing most, a checkered shirt, khaki pants, boots that zipped up the side, a flat cap. We exchanged these for a hospital gown while nurses assessed his needs.

Most nights during those two weeks I drove about an hour to visit after work, then returned home in the dark. My father was steadily declining, becoming less present with us. We were keeping vigil, waiting. Yet we were not waiting for someone to arrive; we were waiting for my father to leave.

There is a ritual in more "high church" or liturgical traditions following the Maundy Thursday service called the "stripping of the altar". All of the remaining candles, the chalice of wine, the paten that held the bread, the cloth over the table, *everything* is removed. If there is a cross in the space, it is covered. There is emptiness.

Even the "reserve sacrament", the leftover bread and wine that were blessed during the Maundy Thursday service, is taken to a different location called the Altar of Repose. In our congregation, people will sign up for shifts to sit vigil with this bread and wine, simply sitting, and waiting.

Several years ago, just a few years after my father's death, I decided that I would spend the entire night there, at the church, near the altar of repose. When I was not in the room with the bread and wine, I slept on a pew in a sleeping bag. Lying on the pew reminded me of evening services as a child, with my head resting in my mother's lap. The service was likely a revival, one of those particularities of Evangelical churches, services every night of the week, generally with an emphasis on rousing those who were asleep in their faith.

That morning I awoke at about five. I rolled up my sleeping bag. Took it and my pillow to my car. I brushed my teeth at the sink in the church bathroom, reminding me of sleeping in many churches/homeless shelters during my time in Richmond. Then I walked.

I was not sure where I was going as I gathered my belongings. A woman who had been keeping vigil at the sacrament said that they were thinking that they might go. She asked if I was staying. I told her that I was. And then she said quizzically, "You can't help it; it draws you in."

She went back inside the room with the altar. I walked outside into the cool air.

And I walked.

The campus on which the church sits is an old orphanage, a place where you come if you have no other family to care for you. The grounds are sprawling, with tended gardens. The garden in the center, shaped like a teardrop holds a "double cherry" tree, a dogwood, grass, and chairs. The teardrop guides you around with the largest part closest to the chapel.

It was dark. I could have walked around the campus, even back to where there is a labyrinth. But as it was dark, I kept circling the teardrop, losing count, not caring how many times.

It felt good to feel the cool morning air; birds were beginning to stir. The breeze was quietly stirring the chimes hung on the porch of the parish hall. I walked round and round until I felt stillness again. The vigil had felt like a long expanse of an evening, with sleeping and waking, with minutes feeling like hours, with a stopped feeling to the time, a stillness.

I received the call just after the middle of the day, on Thursday My mother let me know that something had changed, with his breathing; she asked that I come soon. I canceled my patients for the rest of that day and the next, *knowing*. I drove to the facility, walking in the doors, turning right, away from the common area, toward the corner room where my father lay. His breathing was more rapid, shallow, although he did not appear to be in distress. He was no longer communicating at all, with anyone.

There were fewer visitors that evening; it was mostly the three of us sitting together, listening, waiting.

As we readied for "sleep", I lay on a fold-up cot against the wall. My mother had pushed the recliner next to my father's hospital bed. They would sleep side by side, one more time. I would doze in and out, sometimes getting up to walk, returning to lie down again.

And in that stillness, that still point, where minutes felt like hours, where "past and future are gathered", we sat vigil in the emptiness of that room. We waited on death.

Holy Saturday

The days in between my father's death and his burial were measured in moments of silence.

The out-of-town family that would attend did not have far to drive. In our small town, there would be a visitation on the evening before the funeral, the funeral being planned for Sunday afternoon. My father had last attended church two weeks prior, checking into the hospice facility on Monday morning after. He missed the one Sunday in between, only to return to church that Sunday for the last time.

Moments of silence punctuated the conversations with the funeral home director. He would ask us about caskets, vaults, the obituary My mother and I would look at each other, pause, and then break the silence with what we thought he would have wanted.

The Saturday evening of the visitation, there was a low hum to the voices of family and friends, of a church community that surrounded us. The sound of these voices was occasionally punctured by a laugh or hearty greeting. Yet in the midst of the noise, I felt a silence there too.

My daughter walks up to me. I lift her up so that she can see Papa, lying in the casket. She had some of the blue M&Ms that we had given him just a few weeks ago. She placed next to his hand. I do not remember there being words with this gesture.

In the silence, you are allowed to settle into the ground of grief, into the soft dirt that feels your weight, that molds slightly around you. Even as the busyness of voices, of physical embraces, of hands shaken happens with you and around you, the silence is there. That silence is in you, around you, moving through you.

Holy Saturday is a day of silence. Henri Nouwen writes about it as "the day of God's solitude".

For me, the spaces of silence have enabled me to allow limits to be broken. We all have the ability to limit our parents, not seeing them in their fullness. We can make a caricature of particular qualities, while not seeing the other aspects of who they are. The silence allows me to see my father for all that he was.

In the silence too, our limits on God may also be broken. There can be a loneliness to that silence, feeling that the God we knew is gone. But perhaps it is only the limited idea of God that is now gone. The silence allows for something bigger, different, perhaps more true, certainly more honest. Yet, it is like a death, this experience.

Nouwen writes further, "This divine silence is the most fruitful silence that the world has ever known. From this silence, the Word will be spoken again and make all things new."

Perhaps that soft dirt of silence will yield growth, but for a time it is cold and quiet.

Easter

We buried my father on a Sunday afternoon.

The church that he and my mother attended, that I attended through my early adulthood, had expanded and moved to a larger worship space. But my father's service was held in the old space, the "chapel", a space that in my memory still has lime green carpet and white paint on the sides of the pews.

The smaller space was filled with people from the church, but also the other communities with which we were connected. Colleagues from my practice were there. Friends from the church that we now attend were sitting up in the choir loft due to the lack of seating. Throughout the service, in walking over to the cemetery across the road where he would be buried, and after the internment, there was the sharing of stories.

There were stories of my father as a young man and as an adult. There were stories about him as a farmer, as a mechanic, as song-leader in that very church for a while, about how he had helped others when they needed it, about his humor. Up until the last few years, he would still get a glimmer in his eye as he told a joke or gently teased a friend or simply did something that you did not expect at that moment.

These stories broadened my narrow experience of my father, creating a larger, more complete narrative of who he was.

This is what we do, following death. We must tell the story again. And in the telling, the story achieves a fullness that our own particular view, our own particular narrative lacks.

You do not tell the story in the same way on the other side of death. The stories you tell change with an emphasis on some parts and not others. Some people become saints after their death; for some people, you mostly remember the sin. But the story does change.

Part of that change is inside you.

On the other side of death, whether it is the death of a parent or the death of a loved one, *we are changed.* I have to imagine that this is how it was for the disciples, for those women, for Mary, and maybe for Jesus too … on the other side of death.

The readings for Easter in those Christian traditions that observe the Easter Vigil tell the story again, the whole story.

Starting in Genesis the readings speak of the creation of our world, the way that God is in and through and among all of creation; that it is good. There follow a song and a prayer. Next comes Noah and the flood, of the way that God preserves a people, then a song and a prayer. Exodus from Egypt and slavery, the God of deliverance from oppression. Passages from Isaiah and other prophets about salvation being offered for everyone and how there are new beginnings for all of us, even the one whose heart has become hard like stone (Ezekiel 36:24–28). Then follow passages that for Christians prefigure this person of Jesus, his life and his death, and the way in which for Christians we see Christ opening salvation to *everyone.*

You hear all the stories again on the *other* side of death; here, there is new life.

The writers of the gospels seem to hear Jesus's words in a very different way in light of his death. There are phrases such as "he said this to show the way that he would die" among so many other statements that communicate an interpretation and *re-interpretation* following the events of Jesus's death and resurrection.

You tell the story again. You plant seeds and watch them grow.

My father had planted sunflowers in the fields behind that cemetery for years. The earth in which he was buried was land that he had donated to the church cemetery just a few years prior. It was land that he had plowed and planted.

As a last act at the burial, my two children both held sunflowers to add to the spray of flowers on top of the casket. We all solemnly walked toward the raised casket, taking a step up, with me gently lifting them one by one. My daughter went first and delicately laid the sunflower on top of Papa's other flowers.

My son was second.

I lifted him up so he could place the flower. But as I lowered him to the green-carpeted step, he seemed to realize with a glint in his eye that it would be fun to jump from that step to the ground underneath. In that second I could see that humor in him, as it had been with my own father. I set him down on the step and just watched as he balled his fists on both sides, pulled back his arms, and lept to the ground.

www.ingramcontent.com/pod-product-compliance
Lightning Source LLC
Chambersburg PA
CBHW060444040426
42331CB00044B/2596